The New Crochet

The New Crochet

40 Wonderful Wearables

LARK BOOKS

A Division of Sterling Publishing Co., Inc.
New York

Technical Editor: Marilyn Hastings
Art Directors: Stacey Budge and Kathleen Holmes
Cover Designer: Barbara Zaretsky
Assistant Editor: Nathalie Mornu
Associate Art Director: Shannon Yokeley
Editorial Assistance: Delores Gosnell
Photography: Stewart O'Shields
Illustrations: Orrin Lundgren
Hair and Makeup: Diane Chambers

Library of Congress Cataloging-in-Publication Data
Taylor, Terry, 1952-
   The new crochet : 40 wonderful wearables / Terry Taylor.—1st ed.
      p. cm.
   Includes index.
   ISBN 1-57990-686-9 (hardcover)
   1. Crocheting—Patterns.   I. Title.
TT820.T365 2005
746.43'40432--dc22

10 9 8 7 6 5 4 3 2 1

First Edition

Published by Lark Books, A Division of Sterling Publishing Co., Inc. 387 Park Avenue South, New York, N.Y. 10016

© 2005, Lark Books

Distributed in Canada by Sterling Publishing, c/o Canadian Manda Group, 165 Dufferin Street Toronto, Ontario, Canada M6K 3H6

Distributed in the U.K. by Guild of Master Craftsman Publications Ltd., Castle Place, 166 High Street, Lewes, East Sussex, England BN7 1XU Tel: (+ 44) 1273 477374, Fax: (+ 44) 1273 478606, e-mail: pubs@thegmcgroup.com, Web: www.gmcpublications.com

Distributed in Australia by Capricorn Link (Australia) Pty Ltd., P.O. Box 704, Windsor, NSW 2756 Australia

If you have questions or comments about this book, please contact:

Lark Books, 67 Broadway, Asheville, NC 28801 (828) 253-0467

Manufactured in China

ISBN 1-57990-686-9

For information about custom editions, special sales, premium and corporate purchases, please contact Sterling Special Sales Department at 800-805-5489 or specialsales@sterlingpub.com.

Contents

Introduction

WHAT DO YOU THINK of when you hear the word crochet?

Do images of ruffled, lacey doilies and antimacassars in a great aunt's living room appear in your head? (Does anyone even know what an antimacassar is any more?)

Or do you envision models parading down the fashion catwalks—right now—in New York, Paris, and Milan? Models sporting shoulder-hugging wraps in soft-as-a-kiss mohair, intricate-looking (but easy to make) faux suede belts, and feminine silk ribbon tanks and ponchos?

If you're of the latter point of view, *The New Crochet* is the book you've been waiting for. Are you a knitter looking for different ways to work with luscious yarns? Did you crochet 30 years ago and yearn to pick it up again? (Yes, Granny Squares are back. But there's so much more to do!) Or are you someone looking for a needlecraft that's easy to learn, portable, and will give you results you'll be proud of?

The New Crochet is filled with timeless and of-the-times wearables that are a pleasure to wear or to make for someone else to show off. There are simple projects that you can work up in an evening or two, as well as more complex projects that may take several evenings to finish.

If you already know how to crochet—even if it's been a while—you have my permission to skip the basics section. Go ahead: Grab a hook, gather some scrumptious yarns, and start in on the project of your choice. Don't remember what a triple treble is? No problem: Refer back to crochet basics to refresh your memory. It will all come rushing back to you.

However, if you've never picked up a crochet hook and thought that crochet was too hard to learn, let me disabuse you of that notion. Crochet isn't as tedious or as complex as it might appear to be. I promise.

Can you hold a pencil, competently count (I'm not kidding, counting can be important), and spare a little time to practice? If you can do those three things, you'll be able to crochet most of the projects in this book.

All of the stitches you need to know are explained and illustrated step-by-step in the basics section. I taught myself how to crochet simply by following the printed instructions in a crochet book. You can too. Really. With the popularity of knitting and crochet these days, there's an excellent chance you know someone to turn to for advice. Don't be afraid to ask and, more importantly, don't be afraid to just start crocheting on your own.

To start, choose a couple of simple stitches, such as the chain stitch and single crochet, and practice making those stitches with any type of yarn you might have stashed away. Make a sample of those stitches, nothing more than a practice piece. You may feel awkward to begin with (I did) but don't give up. As you practice you'll begin to develop a feel for making stitches, making them even, and you'll see that crochet isn't that difficult to do. Once you feel comfortable making those easy stitches, look for a project that features them and dive right in.

You might want to start with a classically elegant mohair shawl, a simple rectangle that's worked in one simple stitch (page 85). Next, try your hand at working in the round with a head-hugging cloche that works up on the double (page 55). After you've mastered one or two easy projects, you'll have gained enough confidence (and have gathered enough compliments!) to move on to more complex projects.

There are enough projects in this book—easy to advanced—to fill your closet if you have the time. Crochet them with the yarns that the designer used or be bold and use yarns that you've chosen (there's a section on page 10 that tells you how to substitute yarn types). Add your own special touches—buttons, fringe, or beads—to satisfy your creative urges and fashion flair.

Crochet isn't just Granny Square afghans or antimacassars (have you looked up that word yet?). It's the newest trend in fiber crafts that's popular with newcomers to the craft and veteran needleworkers alike. It's fashionable, fun, and satisfying. Grab a hook, some yarn, and give it a try.

Crochet Basics

Tools

One of the chief pleasures of crochet—aside from working with wonderful yarns—is that you need relatively few tools to accomplish the work. Aside from yarn, you simply need a hook. That's it! Of course, there are always additional tools that are handy and helpful to have, but not essential.

The Hook

Long ago, crochet hooks were made of hand-carved wood, bone, or even ivory. Today hooks are most commonly made of aluminum, plastic, or steel, although you can still readily purchase wooden hooks with decoratively turned handles or light-as-a-feather bamboo hooks in specialty yarn shops. If you're so inclined, you can even seek out bone and ivory hooks in antique shops and online auctions. Aluminum, plastic, and wooden hooks are normally used with all types of yarns; steel hooks, with fine threads.

A crochet hook—no matter what material it's made of—has five basic parts, each with a specific function (figure 1). The point of the hook (a) is used to insert the hook into stitches. The throat (b) grabs the yarn to pull it through a stitch. The diameter of the shaft (c) helps determine the size of your stitches. It holds the loop or loops you're working with. The thumb rest (d) gives your fingers and thumb a flat area to grasp firmly as you work. The handle (e) is used for balance or leverage.

In the directions for each project in this book and for any other crochet pattern you might work on, you'll be instructed to use a specific hook size. Whether you use aluminum, plastic, or wooden hook is a matter of personal preference. What matters is the size of the hook—it determines the stitch size and, to some extent, the gauge (number of stitches per inch) that the pattern is based on.

You will encounter three different systems of hook sizes when you start to amass a working collection of hooks. The Continental (European) system uses millimeters, the U.S. (American) system uses a combination letter/number system, and the United Kingdom uses a numeric system. The hook sizes listed in the projects are of the Continental and U.S. systems (page 142).

Additional Tools

Scissors, especially small ones with sharp points, are indispensable tools. Breaking yarn is not an efficient way to cut yarn. Always use scissors.

Stitch markers are handy when you need to mark the end of a row in your work or a specific stitch within a row. If you don't wish to purchase stitch markers, use a safety pin or a short length of contrasting yarn to mark your spot.

Rulers and cloth tape measures with

Figure 1

both standard and metric measurements are useful tools that you probably already have. You will use these tools to measure your work as you progress, to check your gauge (see page 13), and to measure finished pieces as you finish and block them.

Rustproof pins of all types—straight pins, T-pins, and safety pins—all have their uses. Make absolutely sure that any type of pin you choose to use is rust-proof. T-pins are useful for blocking (see page 27) and safety pins can be used as stitch markers. Straight pins are great for securing crocheted pieces together as you stitch them and later as you block them.

Tapestry needles with large eyes and blunt points are necessary for finishing a completed crochet project. Using a plastic or metal needle is a matter of preference. Use them to weave loose yarn ends back into your stitches, or to sew together the seams of a garment.

Bags make it easy for you to take your crochet anywhere and everywhere you go. You may choose to tuck your current project, yarn, and a few tools in a plastic grocery bag or invest in a stylish, multipurpose needlework tote. Just be sure your bag doesn't have any tiny holes your hooks or pins might slip through.

Yarn

Variety, luxury, and novelty are some of the buzzwords you encounter when reading about yarn today. The range of different types of yarn is, simply put, mind-boggling. If you've never shopped for yarn you may easily be overwhelmed as you look for material for a specific project (pleasantly so, I might add). Give in to the addictive pleasure of acquisition; don' t resist it! After all, you can always find a way to use it sooner or later.

Each project in this book lists a generic yarn type to use. In addition, each project lists the manufacturer, style, and color of the specific yarn used to create the project. Pay attention to the type of yarn specified for each project and, if you wish to use a yarn other than the one the designer used (see Substituting Yarn on page 10), look for that type of yarn.

For our purposes, yarn or thread are catchall terms for any fiber-like material we use for crochet, even if we're crocheting with ribbon, cloth, or other materials.

Yarn Types

In general, yarns—both natural and synthetic—are grouped into types classified by weight or size (yarn thickness). There is some crossover between types, but in general they are separated into six distinct groups.

Super Fine yarn is commonly referred

to as fingering or sock weight yarn. It's the thinnest of yarn types. It's also referred to as baby weight and used to make delicate, lightweight garments for, you guessed it, babies.

Fine yarns are medium weight yarns used for a wide variety of projects. Sport weight and, sometimes, baby weight are used to describe this type of yarn depending on the manufacturer.

Light yarns are double knitting (DK) weight and light worsted yarns. These are slightly thicker than fine yarns. This common type of yarn can often be used in patterns that call for sport weight yarns, the end result being a slightly heavier fabric.

Medium weight yarns are usually called worsted weight yarns. These readily available yarns are used in many ways. They're the type of yarns you're certain to find in large discount chains or stores that don't offer a wide variety of yarn products.

Bulky weight yarns are also known as chunky, craft, and rug yarns. They work up quickly.

Super Bulky yarns work up even more quickly. If they haven't been spun into a recognizable form of yarn, they may also be referred to as roving.

Novelty Yarns

Novelty yarn is an all-purpose term used to describe all of those glorious, tantalizing yarns that have bumps, bouclé, nubs, or threads that wiggle and dangle. Their underlying structure—unlike strictly spun yarns—can be spun, woven, chained, or knit; their finish can be smooth or brushed. Novelty yarns are dazzling and a real temptation for those of us who are addicted to purchasing yarn. They can be worked alone, worked in tandem with standard types of yarn, or used as decorative accents.

In general, a novelty yarn is either heavier than a bulky or chunky weight yarn or is a thin, almost threadlike yarn. But that doesn't always hold true. Manufacturers have responded to consumer demand and are creating novelty yarns in a wide range of sizes.

Substituting Yarn

Let's imagine that you don't like a particular shade of green used in a scarf pattern or that you're allergic to a specific type of wool called for in a sweater pattern. What do you do? Abandon the project? Certainly not! You can substitute the yarn of your choice for the same type of yarn called for in the pattern.

However, don't imagine that you can substitute bulky yarn for a pattern that calls for fingering yarn. You won't be happy with the results at all. Simply follow the four steps that follow to substitute the yarn of your choice.

First, identify the yarn type that the pattern calls for. If needed, re-familiarize yourself with the different standard yarn types (see page 9). Once you know the type of yarn you need, look for a similar type of yarn that suits your needs and desires.

Second, determine how much yarn the project requires. Jot down the total length of each ball of the original yarn in the pattern. Multiply the number of balls called for by yards/meters per ball. This will tell you how much yarn you will need. Write down the total amount of each yarn type you will need for the project.

Third—and here's the fun part—go shopping! When you have found the yarn you want to use, divide the total yardage you need by the yards/meters per ball of your new yarn. Round up to the next whole number (you don't want to find yourself running short of yarn!). This will give you the number of skeins you'll need of the substitute yarn.

Finally, crochet a gauge sample with the recommended hook and the yarn you've purchased. Don't skip this step (see Gauging Success on page 13). If the gauge is accurate, crochet away!

The Pattern:
Your Road Map to Success

I hope you've thumbed through this book and thought to yourself: I'd like to make that! And that! So how do you go about making that project? It's easy; you gather the materials and follow the pattern instructions.

Written patterns give you a lot of important information *before* you actually pick up your hook and yarn. Reading a pattern from beginning to end before you crochet isn't an optional step; it's required, and simply makes sense. Even experienced crocheters do it. Think of it as if you were sitting down with a road atlas before embarking on a long road trip: It's easy to map out where you're going and how to get there before you leave the house—a whole lot easier than attempting to whip out the map and read it in eight lanes of speeding, rush hour traffic in a strange city!

Let's take a look at what you can expect to learn from crochet patterns in this book or any other book or magazine.

Experience Level
A pattern will tell you which level of experience it's designed for: beginner, easy, intermediate, or experienced. Pay attention to the level of experience needed to create a project, then read through the pattern just to be sure it's right for you.

Beginners will use basic stitches in a straightforward manner.

There will be minimal shaping of the project.

Easy patterns use basic stitches, simple repetitive stitch patterns, simple color changes, and easy-to-master shaping and finishing techniques.

Intermediate patterns use a variety of stitches and more complex stitch patterns. Lace patterns and complex color changes may also be used.

Experienced level patterns will use intricate stitch patterns, work from charted stitches, use finer threads, smaller hooks, and detailed shaping and finishing.

Size or Dimensions
A pattern will give you the finished dimensions of a project or provide you with the size ranges that can be made with the pattern.

Materials and Tools
Every pattern will list the materials, the specific hook size, and other tools that you'll need. The pattern will tell you exactly which type of yarn is used and approximately how much you'll need to create the project. In most cases, the pattern will tell you the specific brand of yarn used to crochet the project.

Stitch List
The stitches used in the pattern will be listed. If advanced or specialty stitches are used, you'll be given directions for the stitches. These stitches will be

listed in abbreviated form to save space (see chart on page 142). If special changes in standard stitch construction or unique working methods are used, those changes will be noted and brought to your attention before you start.

Gauge
There will be a gauge specified for the design. Pay attention to the gauge. If you want your project to be the size you intend it to be, make a gauge sample. Read Gauging Success on page 13 for more information on creating a gauge sample.

Instructions, Pattern Notes, and Graphs

Every pattern will be written with step-by-step instructions for each and every row you crochet. (Really.) It will begin with the number of chain stitches you need for your foundation row, then continue with a row-by-row description of the stitches or pattern stitches needed to complete the project. If the project is made with several pieces, each piece will be given separate step-by-step directions.

If there are special stitch variations or unusual working methods for the pattern, these will be noted in a separate section of pattern notes or working notes.

If there are specific color changes that make up a pattern for checks or stripes, these changes may be shown graphically with an illustration or a charted graph. Each square on a charted graph will be equal to a given number of stitches.

When a garment is made up of one or more pieces, you may be given a diagram that shows the dimensions of each piece needed to create the project.

Finishing and Assembly

Finally, if your project needs to be blocked (shaped) or assembled, the instructions will tell you what to do and, in some cases, how to do it.

In addition, if the project calls for buttonholes, fringe, pompoms, or other embellishments you'll be given instructions on how to create each one as needed.

How to Read a Pattern

Crochet directions are written in a special (but not secret!) language with abbreviations, punctuation marks, and special terms and symbols. They may look mysterious or even forbidding, but with a little practice and a bit of thinking through each direction, you'll soon catch on.

Familiarize yourself with the table of abbreviations on page 142 and refer back to it as often as needed. These standardized abbreviations are commonly used in most crochet instructions around the world. In no time at all, you'll know what hdc means without thinking about it twice.

In addition to abbreviations, you'll need to pay attention to a few special symbols and punctuation marks. They serve a useful purpose when reading crochet directions.

Symbols and Punctuation

* An asterisk is used to shorten instructions. Work all instructions following an * as many times as indicated.

: A colon tells you to stop and pay attention. Usually a number will follow that tells you the number of stitches you should have in that row or round.

( ) Parentheses are often used to enclose a set of steps and to indicate changes for different sizes.

[ ] Brackets will be used to indicate another block of instructions grouped within parentheses.

Speak It to Yourself

1. Read through the directions from beginning to end, row by row, translating each abbreviation into a word or phrase. Then, read the directions aloud.

Yes, it sounds like a silly thing to do, but it works.

2. As you begin to work a specific stitch pattern, make a mantra of the sequence of stitches you need to work. Repeat the mantra to yourself as you make each part of the pattern. After a while, you'll be able to execute the stitch pattern almost without thinking about it.

Gauging Success

You wouldn't want to build a door for your house without measuring the opening first, now would you? The door you build might be too large or too small to fit the opening. You wouldn't be happy putting all of that time, effort, and expense into creating a door that doesn't fit in the intended opening.

How do you ensure that what you crochet matches the size you want for the project? It's simple: Create a gauge sample each and every time, before you start any project. The gauge of any pattern is stated right after the stitches that are used in the project, right along with hook size and yarn type (see Reading a Pattern on page 11).

Gauge is measured by stitches or rows of stitches per inch. If your project is made solely with single crochet, you'll use single crochet stitches to make the sample. If the project has a set of several different stitches that repeat across the row, you'll need to create a sample for that set of stitches. If you're not very experienced with crochet, you may have a few questions about the process.

Why should I make a gauge sample?

It's an excellent way to practice your stitches, and it's the only way to insure your project will be the size you desire. Each and every yarn type differs slightly from manufacturer to manufacturer. In the same way, every person who crochets does so a bit differently. Stitch tension varies from person to person, and from day to day!

How large a sample do I need to make?

In general, people tend to crochet tighter at the beginning and end of rows. You'll want to measure your gauge in the sample where the stitches are most consistent—the center. Create a gauge sample that measures 4 x 4 inches (10 x 10 cm) or larger. It's imperative that you create your sample with the same yarn and hook that you plan to use to crochet the project.

What do I do with the sample?

For the most accurate measurement of your gauge, you need to treat your sample just as you would your finished project. If your pattern calls for blocking the project, you'll need to block the sample square (see page 27). Lay the sample flat to measure and count both the number of individual stitches and rows per inch.

What do I do if my sample doesn't measure up?

If your sample doesn't result in the specified gauge, do not, I repeat, do not throw up your hands and quit. Simply rework a sample with a larger (or smaller) hook size or by adjusting your stitch tension as you crochet until your sample matches the required gauge. It's as simple as that.

Gauge is important. If you want that top or skirt to fit as intended, you need to work on achieving the gauge required before you start in on the project. On the other hand (there's always another side to the coin), gauge is not quite so crucial if you're crocheting a simple scarf or a rectangular shawl where fit is not critical. If gauge isn't critical many designers will simply say so at the start of the pattern.

Basic Crochet Techniques & Stitches

Getting Started

Holding the Hook

There's no specifically right or wrong way to hold a crochet hook—it's a matter of personal preference. Hold your hook in a manner that you find comfortable. You can hold your crochet hook as if you're holding a pencil (figure 2) or as if you're holding a knife (figure 3). With either method, grip the flattened section of the crochet hook.

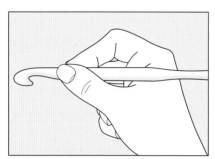

Figure 2

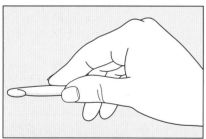

Figure 3

Making a Slipknot

The first step in crochet is to secure the yarn to the hook. You will do this with a slipknot. Create a loop with your yarn. Leave a tail that measures approximately 6 inches (15 cm) and allow the yarn that's connected to the ball to hang down behind the loop (figure 4). Then, use your hook to pull the yarn from your ball of yarn through the loop. Tighten the slipknot by gently tugging on both yarn ends (figure 5). The loop should move easily on the hook without falling off.

Figure 4

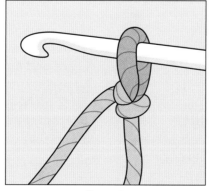

Figure 5

Holding the Yarn

Holding the yarn to maintain an even yarn tension is the most difficult and frustrating part of learning to crochet. Relax. Like all things, you improve with practice, practice, and even more practice. Experts at crochet will tell you that yarn tension varies from person to person, from day to day, and is even influenced by the mood you're in at the moment.

Wrap the yarn counterclockwise around your little finger. Bring the yarn under your ring and middle finger and over your index finger (figure 6).

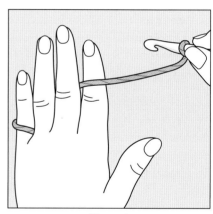

Figure 6

As you start to crochet, grasp the slipknot with your thumb and middle finger. As you lift or lower your index finger, you control the tension of the yarn (figure 7). The yarn should be taut enough that you can easily grab it with the end of the hook, but not so taut that you struggle pulling the yarn and hook through your stitch. An easy way to practice controlling yarn tension without starting a project is to make a simple chain.

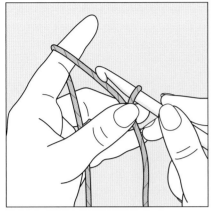
Figure 7

Making a Chain
The foundation of every crochet project is a length of chain stitches (chs). You'll crochet the rows or rounds (rnds) of your project on top of this foundation chain.

Make a slipknot on your hook. Holding your hook, bring the yarn over the hook from back to front. Bring the yarn through the loop (lp) on your hook. At the same time, you'll notice that the loop on your hook has slipped off. You've made one chain!

Be sure to work your chain stitches on the thickest part of the crochet hook between where you grasp the hook and the end of the hook. This will ensure that your stitches are not too tight.

Now repeat that series of steps over and over again. As you make new chain stitches, move your thumb and middle finger—of the hand not holding the hook—up to hold the work (figure 8).

Making a chain is the perfect way to practice maintaining even tension and creating even stitches. You can make a chain and quickly unravel the stitches to start again. With practice, your hands will begin to feel comfortable making the chain. Soon you'll be able to crochet a chain of any length with well-defined chain stitches.

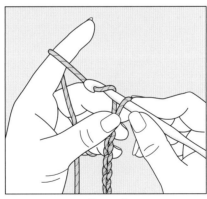
Figure 8

Counting Chain Stitches
The first step of any crochet pattern consists of a foundation chain made of a set number of stitches. As you crochet a foundation chain, it's essential to count the number of stitches in the chain. Jot down the number of stitches when you've finished making a chain, then count them again just to be sure.

You'll notice that your chain has two distinct sides. The front of the chain—the right side (RS)—should appear as a series of well-defined V-shapes. The wrong side (WS) appears as a series of small bumpy loops. Hold the chain with the right side of the chain stitches facing you. Start counting with the last stitch you completed (not the one on your hook) and don't count the slipknot you made at the beginning of the chain (figure 9).

If your stitch count matches the number of chain stitches specified in the pattern, you're ready to crochet.

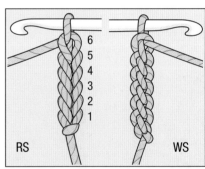
Figure 9

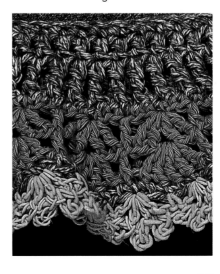

Basic Crochet Stitches

Single Crochet

Single crochet (sc) is a short, basic stitch. To work a row of single crochet stitches, begin with a foundation chain of any number of stitches.

Figure 10

1. Find the second chain stitch from the crochet hook. Insert the point of the hook under the two top loops of the chain stitch (figure 10).

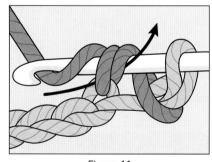

Figure 11

2. Bring the yarn over (yo) the crochet hook, catch the yarn and pull it through the loop on the hook (figure 11). You will now have two loops on your hook.

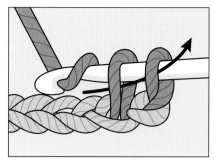

Figure 12

3. Bring the yarn over the hook again, grab the yarn with the hook, and pull the yarn through both loops (figure 12). You've completed your first single crochet stitch.

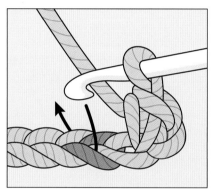

Figure 13

4. Insert your hook in the next chain stitch and repeat the steps to create another single crochet (figure 13).

Turning Your Work

Once you've worked to the end of the first row, you'll need to turn your work around to start the next row of stitches. Rotate your work clockwise if you're holding the hook with your right hand; counterclockwise, if you're holding it with your left hand (figure 14).

Keep the last loop on your hook and turn the completed row so it's under the hand that is holding the yarn. When you do this you'll be able to hold the work between the thumb and middle finger as you work the row.

After you turn the work, you'll need to make a turning chain. A turning chain brings your yarn to the height necessary for the type of stitch you're making in the next row. It will count as the first stitch in the next row.

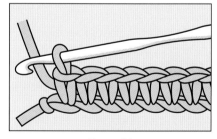

Figure 14

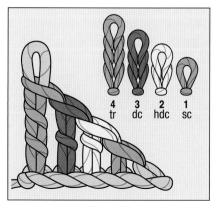

Figure 15

The number of chain stitches you'll need to make for your turning chain depends on what type of stitch you're working in the next row (figure 15).

After you make your turning chain, insert the hook from front to back underneath the top two loops of the stitch specified in the pattern. Crochet across the row as directed in your pattern.

Right Side vs. Wrong Side of the Fabric

As you create your crocheted fabric, it will have a right side (RS) and a wrong side (WS). They look somewhat alike, so how do you tell the difference between the two? Your first complete row of stitches (don't count your foundation chain) is the right side. Another way you can distinguish between the right and wrong sides is to look for the tail of the foundation chain. If you're right handed, the tail of the foundation chain will hang on the left and mark the right side. If you're left handed, the tail of the chain will hang on the right and mark the right side.

Counting Stitches

Don't assume that counting stitches is something only an amateur would do. Even

experts at crochet count their stitches. It's the only way to insure that you're following a pattern exactly.

You already know how to count chain stitches in a foundation chain (see page 15). To count your crochet stitches in a completed row, lay your work on a flat surface. Count the vertical part—the post (P)—of each crochet stitch as shown (figure 16).

It's a good idea to check your stitch count periodically. This is especially true if you're increasing or decreasing the number of stitches in a row (see page 25).

Double Crochet

The double crochet stitch (dc) is the workhorse of crochet. It's about twice as tall as the single crochet stitch. Combining the double crochet stitch with other stitches produces different patterns and textures.

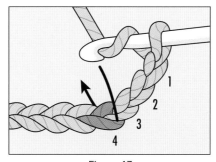
Figure 17

1. Make a foundation chain of any number of stitches. Bring the yarn over the hook and insert the hook into the fourth chain from the hook (figure 17).

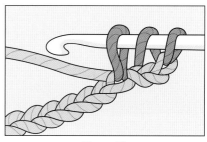
Figure 18

2. Bring the yarn over the hook and pull the yarn through the chain stitch. You'll have three loops on your hook (figure 18).

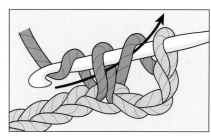
Figure 19

3. Bring the yarn over the hook and draw the yarn through the first two loops on the hook (figure 19). You'll have two loops on your hook.

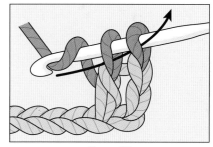
Figure 20

4. Bring the yarn over the hook once more, then pull the yarn through the last two loops on your hook (figure 20). You've completed one double crochet stitch. You'll have one loop left on your hook to start your next double crochet.

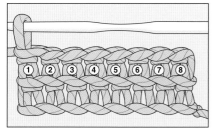
Figure 16

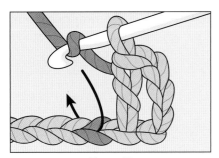

Figure 21

5. Bring the yarn over your hook, insert your hook in the next stitch (figure 21), and continue across the row. At the end of the row, turn your work and chain three to make your turning chain (see figure 15).

Half Double Crochet

The half double crochet (hdc) is used frequently in crochet patterns. It's slightly shorter than a double crochet and taller than a single crochet. To start, make a foundation chain of any number of stitches.

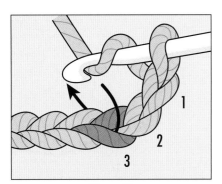

Figure 22

1. Bring the yarn over the hook, locate the third chain stitch from the hook (figure 22), and insert the hook in the chain.

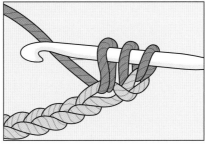

Figure 23

2. Bring the yarn over the hook and catch it with the hook. Pull the hook through the chain. You should have three loops on the hook (figure 23).

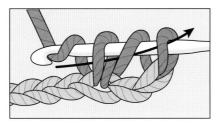

Figure 24

3. Bring the yarn over the hook, catch the yarn with the hook, and pull it through the three loops on the hook (figure 24).

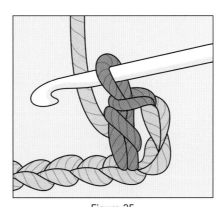

Figure 25

4. You will have one loop left on the hook. You've created one half double crochet stitch (figure 25). Yarn over and insert the hook in the next chain and repeat the sequence across the row.

Treble Crochet

Treble crochet (tr) is taller than double crochet. It's often used to create an open, lacey fabric.

Start with a foundation chain of any number of stitches.

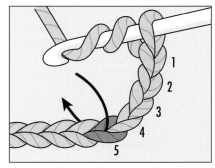

Figure 26

1. Identify the fifth chain stitch from the hook. Bring the yarn over the hook twice (figure 26).

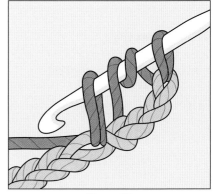

Figure 27

2. Insert the hook into the fifth chain. Bring the yarn over the hook, catch the yarn, and pull the hook through the chain. You'll have four loops on the hook (figure 27).

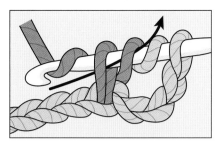

Figure 28

3. Bring the yarn over the hook, catch the yarn, and slide the hook through the first two loops (figure 28).

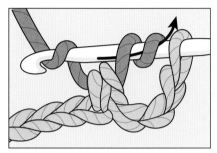

Figure 29

4. Yarn over the hook and draw your yarn through the next two loops on the hook (figure 29).

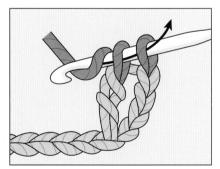

Figure 30

5. Yarn over the hook and draw the yarn through the last two loops on your hook (figure 30).

Figure 31

6. You will end up with only one loop on your hook. You've completed one treble crochet stitch (figure 31). Yarn over twice and repeat the steps in the next chain stitch.

Double Treble

The double treble crochet (dtr) is even taller than a treble crochet. This stitch is best used to create a very loose, openwork fabric.

Make a foundation chain of any number of stitches, then chain five additional stitches for a turning chain.

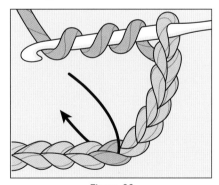

Figure 32

1. Yarn over the hook three times. Insert the hook in the sixth chain from the hook (figure 32). Yarn over the hook.

2. Gently pull the wrapped hook through the center of the stitch carrying the wrapped yarn through the stitch. You will have five loops on your hook.

Figure 33

3. Yarn over the hook. Draw the yarn through the first two loops on your hook. Repeat this step three more times until you have only one loop on the hook. Start your next dtr by bringing the yarn over three times and inserting the hook in the next chain of the foundation row (figure 33).

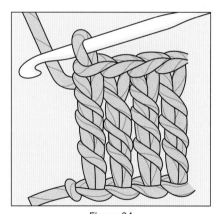

Figure 34

4. At the end of the row (figure 34), make five chains to start another row of dtr.

Slip Stitch

The slip stitch (sl st) is a functional stitch with many, many uses. Use this stitch to create a firm finished edge or to join two finished crocheted pieces (see page 29). You can use a slip stitch to join a new skein of yarn to your crochet project or when you change yarn color. Combine the slip stitch with other stitches to form fancy, complicated-looking stitches. The slip stitch can even be used to create the look of embroidery on crocheted work simply slip stitching across the surface.

As versatile as it is, the slip stitch is most commonly used to join one end of a foundation chain to the opposite end, forming a ring. The ring then forms the foundation for working pieces in the round (see page 26).

To create a slip stitch, insert the hook into any stitch. Bring the yarn over, catch the yarn, and pull the hook through the stitch and the loop on your hook (figure 35). This completes one slip stitch. You'll have one loop remaining on the hook.

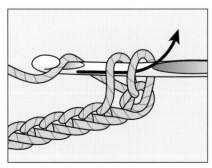

Figure 35

Special Stitches

The following stitches are not used in every project but are useful stitches to know and fun to experiment with. Refer to this section if the pattern you're working calls for any of these special stitches.

Tunisian Crochet

Tunisian crochet—also called tricot crochet, railroad knitting, or Afghan stitch—is a variation of standard crochet with two primary differences.

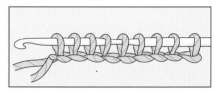

One difference between standard crochet and Tunisian crochet is the size of the hook used: A much longer hook is used to create the work (see photo) because in Tunisian crochet you work a single row in two parts. As you work the first part of each row, the loops you make are kept on the hook (that's why you use a longer hook). Working the second part of the row takes the loops off your hook. The fabric created with Tunisian crochet has a distinctive look that differs from standard crochet.

Tunisian Simple Stitch

Tunisian simple stitch (Tss) is begun with a foundation chain of ordinary chain stitches (see page 15).

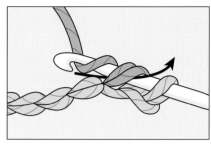

Figure 36

1. Insert your hook into the second chain from the hook (figure 36). Bring the yarn over the hook and draw the yarn through. You will have two loops on your hook.

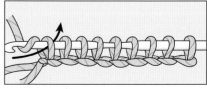

Figure 37

2. Insert your hook into the next chain, bring the yarn over, and draw the yarn through. You've added another loop to your hook. As you work you'll have one loop on your hook for each chain stitch in your foundation chain (figure 37).

Figure 38

3. To work the second half of the row, bring the yarn over the hook and draw it through one loop on the hook (figure 38).

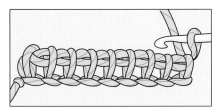

Figure 39

4. Bring the yarn over the hook; draw it through the next two loops on the hook. Bring the yarn over again, draw it through two loops. Continue across the row until only one loop remains on the hook (figure 39).

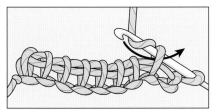

Figure 40

5. To start your next row, insert your hook behind the next vertical bar in the row below (figure 40). Bring the yarn over the hook and draw the yarn through the stitch. Continue across the row, keeping all the loops on your hook (figure 41).

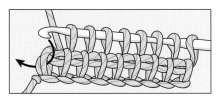

Figure 41

6. Work the return row as you did in steps 3 and 4: Bringing the yarn first through one loop, then completing the row by bringing the yarn through two loops at a time across the row.

Tunisian Slip Stitch

Tunisian slip stitch (Tsl) is worked in the following manner.

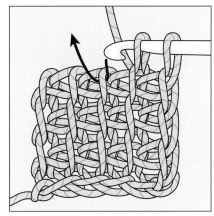

Figure 42

1. Insert the hook into a stitch as you would when you work Tunisian simple stitch, but do not yarn over or pull the yarn through the stitch (figure 42).

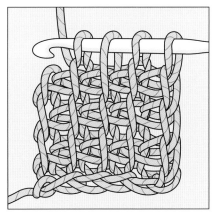

Figure 43

2. Continue with your next stitch, working it in the usual manner by bringing the yarn over and pulling the yarn through the loop. The slipped stitch will remain on the hook. Note the longer appearance of the vertical bar (figure 43).

Finger Crochet

It's possible to crochet without using a hook! Have you had a carpenter working on your home lately and noticed their long, chained extension cords? They don't call it crochet, but that's what it is.

Single crochet and double crochet stitches are easily made using your fingers. It's a fun way to whip up a simple scarf or even a hat. Working this way may not be your cup of tea, but it's easy to do with a bulky yarn. Simply do not even entertain attempting this technique with any other yarn type: You'll drive yourself to distraction!

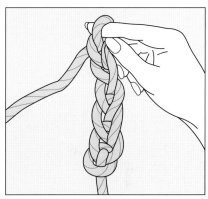

Figure 44

1. Make a slipknot to hold the first loop. Hold the slipknot with one hand and insert your forefinger through the loop. Draw the yarn through the loop to create your first stitch (figure 44).

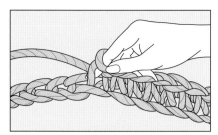

Figure 45

2. At the end of the chain, turn your work and work back across the row using your forefinger as a "hook" to draw the yarn through a loop (figure 45).

Reverse Single Crochet

Just as the name implies, you work this stitch just as you do a regular single crochet—except in reverse. You work this stitch from left to right. This stitch is used most frequently for creating a finished edge on your completed work.

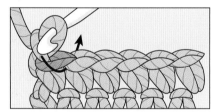

Figure 46

1. Work this stitch with the right side of your work facing you. Insert the hook from front to back in the stitch to the right of your hook (figure 46).

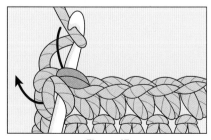

Figure 47

2. Bring the yarn over the hook and pull the yarn through the stitch (figure 47).

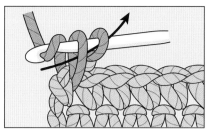

Figure 48

3. Yarn over and bring the yarn through both loops. You've completed one reverse single crochet (figure 48). Continue to work back across the row and fasten off the yarn at the end of the row (see page 26).

Loop/Fur Stitch

This stitch is simply another variation of single crochet. It is usually worked on "wrong side" rows because the loops form at the back of the crocheted fabric. The long loops that are created make an interesting looped fabric. If desired, you can cut the loops to subtly change the texture of the fabric.

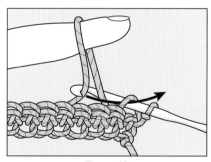

Figure 49

1. Use the left-hand finger to control the size of the loop. Insert the hook, pick up both threads of the loop, and draw them through (figure 49).

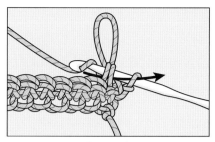

Figure 50

Figure 51

2. Wrap the yarn over the hook (figure 50) and draw through all of the loops on the hook to complete the stitch (figure 51).

Useful Stitch Techniques

You don't have to work crochet stitches in the same way, over and over again. The techniques explained here are used in many different ways: to give different looks to familiar stitches, to change the shape or colors of the piece you're crocheting, or to give you another method for creating crochet.

Crochet Anatomy

Crocheted fabric is composed of stitches and spaces of varying sizes. A completed stitch is composed of the front loop, back loop, and the post.

As you work a crochet pattern, you may be directed to work into or around different parts of a stitch or even into the spaces between stitches. These subtle differences in working methods will change the look of the stitch and the finished crochet fabric.

Back and Front Loops

As a general rule, a stitch is worked into *both* top loops of your stitching row; doing so gives you a smooth fabric. Inserting a hook into only the front loop (FL) or back loop (BL) of a stitch creates fabric with a ribbed or ridged look (figure 52). You'll be given specific instructions in your pattern if you're to work into front or back loops.

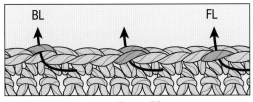
Figure 52

Back and Front Post

You can also create raised patterns—resembling ribbing or even intricate cables—with a post stitch. The way you insert your hook around a post— back post (BP) or front post (FP)— determines the look of the stitch. You'll be given specific instructions in your pattern if you need to use this technique to create a stitch (figures 53 and 54).

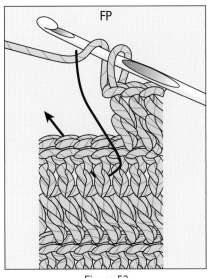
Figure 53

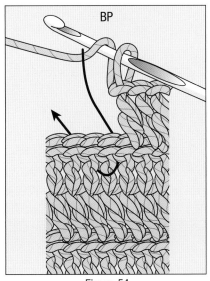
Figure 54

Changing Yarn or Color

Crochet might become boring if you were allowed to use only one color or one type of yarn to create a project. And imagine how difficult it would be if you had to use one—and only one—continuous thread to crochet. It would certainly make crochet a less portable craft.

Should you run out of thread or want to change colors or yarns while you're working, never join a new thread with a knot—it's messy and not an effective way to do it. Whenever possible, it's best to work in a new strand of yarn at the end of a row. So, if you see your yarn diminishing or you think that you may not have enough to finish another row, change your yarn at the end of that row.

Stop just before the last stitch in the row. If you're working in double crochet, work the stitch to the point where you have two loops left on your hook. Drop

the old color and wrap the cut end of the new yarn from back to front (figure 55).

Draw the new yarn through the two loops on your hook. Tug on the end of the old yarn to tighten up the stitch. After tightening the stitch, pick up your new color and make your next stitch. If you plan to pick up the first color again right away, read the section on changing colors and carrying your yarn.

If you don't plan to use the first color again right away, remove your hook from the loop, cut off the first color, leaving a tail to weave in later (see page 26). Insert your hook into the center top of the last double crochet (as shown) down through the center of the stitch (figure 56). Yarn over with the first color's tail; draw the tail up through the stitch. Place the loop of the second color back on the hook and begin your next row with the second color.

Changing Colors
Carrying the Yarn

When a pattern is made up of two or more colors, it would certainly be frustrating to have to change colors every few stitches in the manner described above. You would have a great many yarn ends to weave in when you finished your fabric. However, if you're working on a specific pattern that switches colors often (such as the project on page 134), there's an easier way.

With this method you carry a strand of color across the tops of your stitches in the previous row. It's not unlike working over the end of the yarn when you join a new strand of yarn or color. You lay the unused color of yarn across the tops of the stitches in the previous row and crochet over them (figure 57).

To return to the color you have carried, pull the carried color through the last loops of the color you're working to finish the stitch.

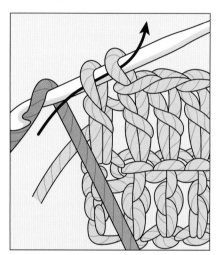

Figure 55

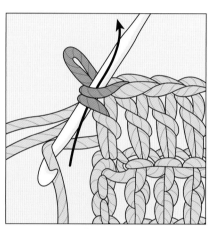

Figure 56

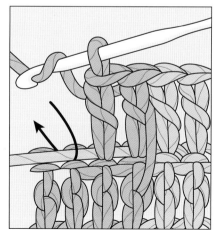

Figure 57

Techniques for Shaping

Working only a rectangle or circle of crochet could be mind numbing and not very useful. There are only so many things you can do with either of those shapes. Simply by adding or subtracting the number of stitches in a row, you can shape the fabric you're creating.

It's very important to count stitches as you increase or decrease according to your pattern (see page 17). Take time to count your stitches, and then count them again!

Increasing

Increasing stitches are simply added stitches worked into a row. Your pattern will tell you when and where to increase (inc). It may be at the beginning, end, or even the middle of the row you're working on. No matter where the increase appears, simply working a given number of stitches into one stitch makes an increase.

Working an increase at the beginning or end of a row is the most common method to add stitches: It gives your fabric a smooth edge. In the example shown, a double crochet increase is worked into the first stitch (figure 58). (Remember: Your turning chain counts as the first stitch!) Figure 59 illustrates a double crochet increase in the middle of a row.

Decreasing

Decreasing is simply subtracting stitches. A decrease (dec) can be worked at the beginning, end, or middle of a row. Your pattern will tell you precisely where and how to make a decrease. In short, you combine two separate stitches into one stitch.

Read your pattern directions carefully so you understand how to work decreases successfully.

For a decrease in double crochet, work a double crochet until you have two loops on your hook. Yarn over your hook and insert it in the next stitch. Yarn over, draw the yarn through the stitch, yarn over and draw the yarn through the first two loops on your hook. Yarn over and draw the yarn through all three loops on your hook.

In the example shown (figure 60), a decrease has been worked in double crochet. If you look at the tops of the stitches, you will see only one stitch crossing the top of two stitch posts.

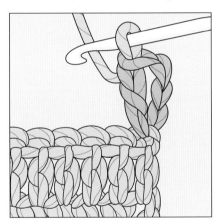

Figure 58

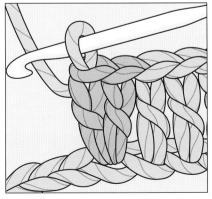

Figure 59

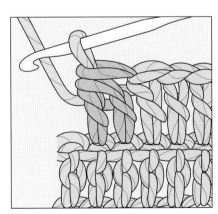

Figure 60

Working in the Round

Working crochet in the round is not any more difficult than working back and forth in straight rows. As you work in the round, you will need to increase the number of stitches in each row in order to go around the widening circumference of the circle or length of a tube. Crochet patterns will specify precisely how many stitches you need to use for each round of the pattern.

To crochet in the round, you'll need to create a center ring as a foundation for your stitches. The most common way to do this is to make a chain of any number of stitches, then join the two ends of the chain with a simple slip stitch (see page 20).

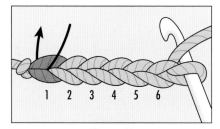
Figure 61

1. Create a chain as specified in your pattern. In this example, it's a chain of six (figure 61).

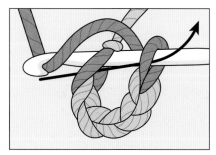
Figure 62

2. Insert your hook into the slip-knot you made, and bring the yarn over the hook (figure 62).

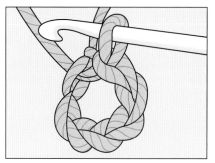
Figure 63

3. Pull the yarn through the stitch and through the loop. The foundation ring is completed (figure 63).

After you've made your ring, you can begin to work your first round. The easy part of crocheting in the round is that you'll usually (but not always) make your first stitches into the center of the ring. If you're creating a tube form, you'll work directly into the foundation chain stitches.

It's necessary to mark the beginning of each round with a stitch marker. Otherwise, you won't easily be able to identify where one round begins or ends. The marker can be a commercially made marker, a length of yarn, or even a paper clip.

Working in the round is also one way to begin a Granny Square (see page 124). And how does a circle become a square? Your pattern will tell you how to make the foundation circle into a square by adding chain loops into your row to create the corners of the square.

Finishing Touches

You've made your very last stitch in a project, but you're not finished yet! As you look at your finished piece you'll see that edges may be curled or the piece is slightly misshapen. Here are the techniques you'll need to finish off your project.

Fastening Off

When you've come to the end of your pattern and made your very last stitch, you'll need to cut your skein of yarn from the crocheted fabric. If you don't fasten the yarn properly, the sight of unraveling stitches will dismay you.

Cut the yarn about 6"/15cm from the hook. Draw the end of the yarn through the last loop on your hook (figure 64). Pull the tail of the yarn gently to tighten the loop. This will prevent the accidental unraveling of your stitches.

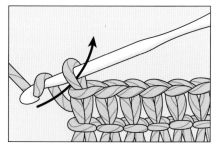
Figure 64

Weaving in the End(s)

Thread a large-eyed tapestry needle with the tail of your yarn end. Weave the yarn through three or four stitches (figure 65). To secure the weaving, weave back through the same stitches. Cut the yarn close to—but not up against—the crocheted fabric. Gently pull the fabric, and the yarn end will disappear into the stitches.

Weave in other yarn ends that you have on the wrong side of your fabric in the same way.

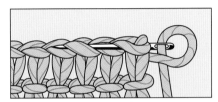

Figure 65

Blocking

As you crochet the piece you are working on, it may become a little misshapen. It may not look like a perfect rectangle, precisely match the dimensions of the pattern, or the edges may be curled. Don't panic. All that's needed is a little gentle persuasion, a process known as blocking. With very few tools and a little effort, you can block an item to the shape that is desired or needed.

First and foremost, you'll need a flat, padded surface to work on. Some good choices: an ironing board, a mattress in the guest room, or a large piece of heavy cardboard slipped inside a large plastic trash bag. The size of your project will dictate the size of padded surface you need. Cover any flat surface with a sheet of plastic or a large trash bag to prevent moisture from damaging the surface. If needed, use a stack of several absorbent bath towels to pad your flat surface. You'll need the padding in order to stick pins into the padded surface to hold your work.

In addition to a flat surface to work on, you'll need the following simple tools to steam or spray block an item:

- ☐ Rust-proof T-pins or straight pins
- ☐ Steam iron
- ☐ Spray bottle
- ☐ Tape measure or ruler

Steam Blocking

Steam blocking is used to lightly block an item that has curling edges or one that is slightly misshapen.

1. Set your iron to a temperature that is compatible with the fiber content of your yarn. If in doubt about the fiber content, use a medium-low setting.

2. Lay your item flat on a padded surface. Lightly tug at the item to bring it into the shape desired. Use pins to hold the item to the desired shape on the padded surface. Check your measurements with a tape measure if needed.

3. Hold your heated steam iron about an inch above the fabric and steam the item. Don't press the iron on the fabric!

4. Allow the item to cool and dry completely before removing the pins.

Spray Blocking

Spray blocking is a little more time-consuming than steam blocking (it takes longer to dry). It's useful if your item is more than a bit misshapen.

1. Lay your item flat on a moisture-protected, padded surface.

2. Gently stretch your item to conform to the correct shape or measurements. Pin the item in place with rust-proof pins.

3. Fill a clean spray bottle with lukewarm water. Spritz the item until it is slightly damp; don't soak it.

4. Smooth the fabric with your hands and pin it with additional pins if the edges are wavy.

5. Allow the crocheted item to dry completely before you remove the pins.

Putting It All Together

Crocheted garments—unless they are crocheted in one piece—have to be assembled after they are blocked. There are several different ways to join garment pieces: You can use different sewing stitches or join them with a crochet hook and yarn.

In the pattern directions each designer has specified the method used to assemble the garment. You may have, or you may develop, a preference for a specific assembling technique. Whatever technique you use, take time and care to put as much effort into assembling the garment as you did making the individual pieces.

Whipstitch

With right sides together, neatly sew through both pieces from back to front through a strand on each piece. Leave a tail of about 6 inches (15 cm) hanging free, and weave in the yarn end after you've finished the seam. Take care to match stitches and rows (figure 66).

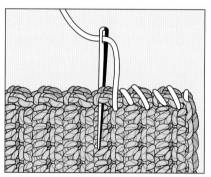

Figure 66

Another method using the whipstitch matches two pieces with wrong sides together. Work through both loops of each stitch of both pieces, inserting the needle from back to front. Leave a tail of yarn at the beginning of the seam and weave the end in when the seam is completed.

One more way to use the whipstitch matches two pieces with wrong sides together. This time, instead of working through both loops, you stitch together only the inside loops of each stitch.

Backstitch

Backstitching creates a sturdy seam. With right sides together, insert the needle from front to back at the seam edge, and then bring it from back to front a half-stitch space forward at 1. Insert the needle back where the stitch began at 2, and bring the needle forward at 3 (figure 67).

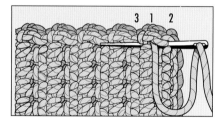

Figure 67

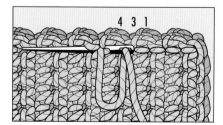

Figure 68

Insert the needle a half stitch back from the yarn at 1 and up again a whole stitch forward at 4 (figure 68). Work your way across the seam. Weave the yarn end in at the end of the seam.

Weaving

With the right sides of both pieces facing you, match the edges stitch for stitch. Sew through both pieces to secure the yarn, and leave a tail to weave in when you finish the seam.

Insert the needle from right to left through one strand on each piece. Bring the needle around and insert it again, from right to left, through the strands (figure 69). Continue to work in this way, tightening the seam edges as you work.

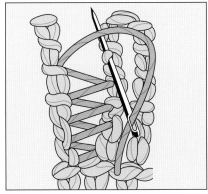

Figure 69

Slip Stitching

Using a crochet hook and yarn to join pieces is a neat method of working. If you work on the wrong side of the piece, a strong seam results. If you work on the right side of a piece, a decorative, embroidered stitch results. If needed, review the slipstitch on page 20.

1. Position two pieces together as directed, with right or wrong sides facing. Take care to be sure that the stitches match across the edge.

2. Work through both pieces using the same size crochet hook you used to crochet the pieces. Insert the hook through the back two loops of the first two stitches. Leave a yarn tail.

3. Yarn over, pull the yarn through. Repeat the stitch in each stitch across the seam (figure 70). Weave in the yarn ends when you have stitched across the seam.

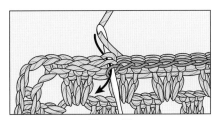

Figure 70

Fringe

Fringe is an easy embellishment to add to any crocheted project you wish. Most patterns include specific directions for fringing your project, but if the urge to add a little fringe to a project that has none strikes you, here's a fool-proof method to use.

Cut a piece of cardboard approximately 4 inches (10 cm) wide and at least 1/2 inch (1 cm) longer than you want your finished fringe to be. Evenly wind your yarn around the cardboard until it is filled, then cut across one end. Set the cut lengths to one side. Continue winding and cutting as needed.

Pick up any number of strands and fold them in half. Working on the wrong side of the fabric, pull the folded end up through a stitch or space and pull the loose ends through the folded end (figure 71). Tighten the knot you've made. Continue working across the edge of the fabric, spacing the fringe as desired. Lay the fringed fabric on a hard surface and trim the yarn ends evenly.

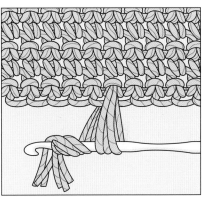

Figure 71

Fashionable Accessories

Head-Hugger Hemp Hat

This cloche-fitting hat (pun intended!) will appeal to everyone who loves a lacey looking topper.

DESIGN BY
Sue McCreary

■ **skill level**
Easy

■ **finished measurements**
This hat is sized to fit most adults.

■ **you will need**
Approx 133yd/120m hemp cord

Hook: 3.5mm/E-4 or size needed to obtain gauge

■ **stitches used**
Chain stitch (ch)

Single crochet (sc)

Double crochet (dc)

Slip stitch (sl st)

■ **gauge**
Take time to check your gauge.

3 sts = 1"/2.5 cm

4 pattern rows = 2"/5cm

Pattern Note
This hat is worked flat from the bottom edge up, then stitched closed.

Pattern
Ch 73.

ROW 1: Sc in 2nd ch from hk and ea ch st across (72 sc). Ch 3, turn.

ROW 2: * Dc next sc. Rep from * across. Ch 1 turn.

ROW 3: Sc in ea dc across ending with sc in top of ch 3. Ch 3, turn.

ROWS 4-11: Rep rows 2 and 3 consecutively.

ROW 12: Dc in next 4 sc, * sk next sc, dc next 5 sc. Rep from * across ending with sk last sc (60dc). Ch 1, turn.

ROW 13: Sc in each dc across ending with sc in top of ch 3. Ch 1, turn.

ROW 14: Repeat row 12 (50dc).

ROW 15: * Place hk in next dc, yo, pull lp thru dc leaving lp on hk. Repeat from * across ending with yo, pull through all lps on hk. Fasten off.

Edging
With RS of hat facing you, attach hemp in beg st, ch 3, sl st in 2nd ch from hk, ch 1, sl st in next st, * sl st in next st, ch 3, sl st in 2nd ch from hk, ch 1, sl st in next st. Rep from * across. Fasten off.

Finishing
Thread a tapestry needle with a length of hemp cord. Use a whip-stitch to sew the seam closed.

This project was created with
1 spool Darice's *20 lb. Hemp Cord* in natural, approx 100g

Baroque Looped Hat

Dr. Zhivago and Lara Antipova would approve of this hat's fashion sensibility. They'd also recognize its ethnic origins from the high windy steppes of Asia. Even if you don't suffer the bitter cold of a Russian winter, you'll warm to its stylish look.

DESIGN BY
Dot Matthews

Pattern Notes

This hat is worked in spiraling rounds: Do not join rounds. Use a stitch marker to indicate first stitch in round, and move it up at the beginning of each round.

Work in back loops (BL) only. Front loops of stitches will be used as directed.

Crown

RND 1: Using color A, ch 2. Work 6 sc in 1st ch (6 sts).

RND 2: Place marker in 1st st. 2 sc in ea st around (12 sts).

RND 3: (2 sc in next st, 1 sc in next st) around (18 sts).

RND 4: (2 sc in next st, 1 sc in next 2 sts) around (24 sts).

RND 5: (2 sc in next st, 1 sc in next 3 sts) around (30 sts).

RND 6: 1 sc in ea st around (30 sts).

RND 7: (2 sc in next st, 1 sc in next 4 sts) around (36 sts).

RND 8: (2 sc in next st, 1 sc in next 5 sts) around (42 sts). Piece measures approximately 6"/15cm across at end of rnd 8.

RND 9: (2 sc in next st, 1 sc in next 6 sts) around (48 sts).

RND 10-21: Sc in ea st around (48 sts). At end of rnd 21, working through both lps, join in 1st sc. Fasten off and weave in end.

Looped Edge

Chain loops are worked in the front loops of the last rnd made before fastening off and in unworked loops of stitches of hat for 6 rnds.

Hold hat with top of crown facing your lap. Attach color B to front loop of last st made before fastening off.

RND 1: (Ch 10, sl st in front lp of next st) around. Place a marker in this loop to mark beg of rnd.

RND 2-6: Work in unworked lps of hat: sl st in next st, (ch 10, sl st in next st) around.

Fasten off and weave in ends.

■ **skill level**

Intermediate

■ **finished measurements**

This hat is designed to fit most adult heads.

■ **you will need**

Color A: 185yd/167m textured bulky yarn in variegated violet

Color B: 60yd/54m eyelash-type bulky yarn in violet

Hook: 5.5mm/I-9 or size needed to obtain gauge

Tapestry needle

■ **stitches used**

Chain (ch)

Single crochet (sc)

Double crochet (dc)

Slip stitch (sl st)

■ **gauge**

Take time to check your gauge.

5 sc and 5 rnds = 2"/5cm

This project was created with

Color A: 1 skein of Lion Brand's *Homespun* in Baroque (322), 98% acrylic/ 2% polyester, 6oz/170g = approx 185yd/167m

Color B: 1 skein of Bernat's *Frenzy* in Ultra Violet (5330), 37% nylon/ 30% acrylic/12% polyester/10.5% alpaca/10.5% mohair, 1.75oz/50g = approx 60yd/54m

Frivolously Fuzzy Felted Bag

This delightful bag will make you smile and add a bright red punch to any ensemble. And it's as practical as it is frivolous—felting the wool in the washing machine gives the bag more heft and strength.

DESIGN BY
Marty Miller

■ skill level

Beginner

■ finished measurements

Size (before felting): approx 14 x 14"/36 x 36 cm

Size (after felting): approx 11 x 12"/28 x 30cm

■ you will need

Approx 380yd/342m worsted weight wool

Approx 198yd/178m eyelash yarn

Hook: 10mm/N/P-15 or size needed to obtain gauge

Tapestry needle

Cloth bag or zippered pillow case

Washing machine

■ stitches used

Chain stitch (ch)

Single crochet (sc)

Slip stitch (sl st)

■ gauge

Because this bag will be felted, gauge isn't critical. The stitches are meant to be loose, and as you are making the bag, check that the measurement of the width of the bag when folded flat is approximately 14"/36cm.

Pattern Notes

The body of the bag is worked holding two strands together. The bag is worked with the right side (RS) out. Join ea round, but do not turn.

The handles are worked in rows, turning ea row.

Body

Hold together one strand of wool and one strand of eyelash yarn, ch 2.

RND 1: 6 sc in 2nd ch from hk, join with sl st to 1st sc. Ch 1.

RND 2: 2 sc in ea sc around, join with sl st. Ch 1.

RND 3: 2 sc in 1st sc, sc in next sc, *2 sc in next sc, sc in next sc, rep from # around (18 sc); join as above. Ch 1.

RND 4: 2 sc in 1st sc, sc in next 2 sc,*2 sc in next sc, sc in next 2 sc, rep from * (24sc); join as above. Ch 1.

RND 5: 2 sc in 1st sc, sc in next 3 sc, *2 sc in next sc, sc in next 2 sc, rep from * around (30 sc); join as above. Ch 1.

RNDS 6–10: Cont to incr 6 sc in same manner, at the end of rnd 10 you will have 60 scs; join as above. Ch 1.

RND 11: Sc in ea sc around (60 sc); join as above. Ch 1.

RNDS 12–40 (or until you run out of the eyelash yarn if that occurs before rnd 40): Rep rnd 11: Ch 1, DO NOT FASTEN OFF. You will be starting one half of the handle from this point.

Handle

1st Half

ROW 1: Ch 1, sc in the 1st sc of the last rnd. Sc in ea of the next 9 scs (10 sc). Ch 1, turn.

Frivolously Fuzzy Felted Bag

ROW 2: Sk the 1st sc, sc in ea of the next 9 sc (9sc). Ch 1, turn.

ROW 3: Sk the 1st sc, sc in ea of the next 8 sc (8sc). Ch 1, turn.

ROW 4: Sk the 1st sc, sc in ea of the next 7 sc (7 sc). Ch 1, turn.

ROW 5: Sk the 1st sc, sc in ea of the next 6 sc (6 sc). Ch 1, turn.

ROW 6: Sk the 1st sc, sc in ea of the next 5 sc (5 sc). Ch 1, turn.

ROW 7: Sk the 1st sc, sc in ea of the next 4 sc (4 sc). Ch 1, turn.

ROW 8: Sc in ea sc (4 sc). Ch 1, turn.

ROWS 9–40: Rep row 8. Fasten off, leaving a long tail to sew the handle together in the middle. This half of the handle should measure approximately 17"/43cm in length.

Second Half

On the last rnd of the bag, count 20 sc after the 1st half of the handle. Join your yarn, and rep the directions for the 1st half of the handle.

Finishing

With the long tail, on the wrong side of the handle, whipstitch the handle halves together.

Weave in all the ends.

Felting The Bag

Put the bag in a zippered pillowcase or cloth bag in order to protect your machine from the wool lint. Set the water level on low, and use the hottest water possible. Add a little laundry detergent.

Fill the machine with 1 or 2 old towels or an old pair of jeans to help agitate the bag.

Set the washer for the most agitation. Check the felting process every 5 or 10 minutes by stopping the machine and peeking into the bag or pillowcase. Remove the bag from the machine before the spin cycle.

You will need to repeat the process to fully felt the bag; allow the machine to empty. Repeat the process 1 or 2 times.

When the bag is felted to your satisfaction, rinse it in a sink with cold water and lay it flat on a sweater drying rack; to dry it may take two or more days. Place newspaper or towels in the bag to speed the drying and help shape the bag.

When the bag is just about dry, place it in the dryer on the lowest temperature or air cycle for a few minutes to fluff it.

This project was created with

2 skeins of Brown Sheep Company's *Lamb's Pride Worsted* in Red Baron (M-81), 85% Wool/15% Mohair, 4oz/112g = approx 190yd/171m per skein

2 skeins Idena's *Happy* in red (#721), 100% Polyester, 1.75oz/50g = approx 99yd/89m per skein

Color Blocks Bracelet

This chunky bracelet is the perfect way to play with a uniquely personal color palette. Crochet one for yourself and you'll be besieged with requests to make more in "their" favorite color combos.

DESIGN BY
Paula Gron

Color Blocks Bracelet

Pattern Notes

You may need to adjust the number of blocks to fit your wrist. This is easily done by adding or subtracting a block. Try the bracelet on for size after the fifth block by wrapping it around your wrist. You'll be able to determine if the bracelet will need one or two more blocks to fit.

Color Block Squares

Block 1

Ch 10 of 1st choice color, turn.

*Insert hk in 2nd chain from hk for 1st sc stitch. Sc across ch, turn, ch 1, sc in ea sc across, turn. Rep from * for 6 more rows.

Draw yarn through lp, leave a 1"/2.5cm tail, and cut.

Block 2

Attach next color choice to last st of prev block with sl st.
Ch 1, and sc in all lps of prev color row, turn.

*Ch 1, insert hk in 2nd sc from hk for 1st sc stitch. Sc across row, turn, rep from * for 6 more rows.

Draw yarn through lp, leave a 1"/2.5cm tail, and cut.

Blocks 3–7

Rep color block 2 for rem colors until you have made enough squares to wrap around your wrist.

Color Rings

Each block will have a contrasting color ring.

Ring 1

*Sc 10 sts around the cabone ring with 1st color choice.

On 11th stitch center the ring on the 1st square and catch under the ring and into a horizontal lp of 1 of the middle 2 sts of the next to last row on the square (figure 1).

Draw lp through and finish the sc. Repeat into 2nd st of that row. Draw lp through and finish the sc.

Sc 10 more sts around ring. Catch under the ring and into a horizontal loop of one of the middle 2 sts of the 1st row of the square.

Draw lp through and finish the sc. Repeat into next middle st of that row. Draw lp through and finish the sc * (approx 24 st).

Draw loop through and fasten off leaving a 2"/5cm tail.

Rings 2–7

Cont as for 1st ring with rem colors. Rep from *, centering the ring and attaching the 11th and 12th scs into horizontal lps as directed. Draw lp through and fasten off leaving a 6"/15cm tail.

Finishing

With the large eye sewing needle, thread 1 yarn tail and take a couple of stitches into the middle loop of the ring next to it, sewing through to the back as well. Weave thread horizontally through the row on the back side of the square.

Repeat for each yarn tail.

Use matching sewing thread to attach the bracelet bar ends to both ends of the wristband.

This project was created with

1 skein each of DMC's #3 *Perle Cotton*, 100% cotton, in terra cotta (356), light mahogany (402), steel grey (414), avocado (469), very dark beige grey (640), medium beige grey(644), and red copper (918), 16yd/14m

Funky-Dory Hemp Belt

This versatile design worked in a colorful hemp thread is a delightful addition to any casual outfit. If you're looking for something more sophisticated, use a silky or metallic thread instead of hemp. Then cap off the ends with faceted glass beads, a gemstone, or Asian silver beads.

DESIGN BY
Paula Gron

■ **skill level**
  Easy

■ **finished measurements**
  15 rings will make a belt approx 36"/91cm long

■ **you will need**
  Approx 63yd/57m multicolored hemp cord

  2"/5cm diameter cabone rings

  Hook: 5.5mm/I-9 or size needed to obtain gauge

  Assortment of wooden beads

■ **stitches used**
  Chain (ch)

  Single crochet (sc)

■ **gauge**
  Approx 26 sc around each ring

  The gauge for this project is variable, depending on the choice of yarn used.

This project was created with
3 balls of Elements' *Hemp Jewelry Cord* in Rainbow (#1490), approx 21yd/19m ea

Belt Rings

Attach one end of the cord to ring with sc.

Sc 12 times across top of ring. *Pick up next ring and attach cord with sc to 1st ring. Sc 12 times in same direction across the 2nd ring.*

Rep from * to * until all rings (as fitted to waistline) are crocheted halfway around.

Proceed stitching around to complete the last ring attached by stitching approx 13 sc or until you meet the next to the last ring. *Attach with a sc to that next ring and proceed to complete it by doing 12 sc around.* Rep from * to * to complete the other half of all of the rings of the belt.

Finishing

Cut 6 long strands of hemp (approx 1yd/1m) for the fringe. Fold each strand in half.

Catch the fold with crochet hook and pull it through one stitch on an end ring. Bring the ends through the loop and tighten to secure (figure 1). Add two more strands in this manner to the ring. Repeat at the opposite end of the belt.

Add beads to the fringe, knotting them in place.

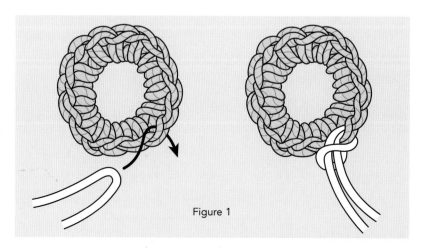

Figure 1

Ooh-La-La Tote

Lacey, yet sturdy enough to haul a baguette and Brie-for-two, this slinky, jewel-tone tote will draw ooh-la-la's from your fellow shoppers.

DESIGN BY
Katherine Lee

Pattern Notes

The tote is worked in the round from bottom up. Bottom is then seamed.

Tote Body

Ch 96, join with a sl st to 1st ch to form ring.

RND 1: Ch 1, 1 sc in ea ch around, join with a sl st to 1st sc (96 sc).

RND 2: Ch 1, 1 sc in 1st sc, *ch 6, sk 5 sc, 1 sc in next sc; rep from * around, join with a sl st to 1st sc (16 ch-6 lps).

RND 3: Ch 1, 1 sc in 1st sc, 7 sc in next ch-6 lp, *1 sc in next sc, 7 sc in next ch-6 lp; rep from * around, join with a sl st to 1st sc.

RND 4 (INC RND): Ch 1, 1 sc in 1st sc, ch 6, sk 2 sc, 1 sc in ea of next 3 sc, *(ch 6, sk 5 sc, 1 sc in ea of next 3 sc) 7 times, ch 6, sk 2 sc, 1 sc in next sc, ch 6, sk 2 sc, 1 sc in ea of next 3 sc, (ch 6, sk 5 sc, 1 sc in ea of next 3 sc) 7 times, ch 6, join with a sl st to 1st sc (18 ch-6 lps).

RND 5: Ch 1, 1 sc in 1st sc, *(7 sc in next ch-6 lp, sk 1 sc, 1 sc in next sc) 8 times, 7 sc in next ch-6 lp*, 1 sc in next sc; rep from * to * once, join with a sl st to 1st sc.

RND 6 (INC RND): Ch 1, 1 sc in 1st sc, *ch 6, sk 2 sc, 1 sc in ea of next 3 sc, (ch 6, sk 5 sc, 1 sc in ea of next 3 sc) 8 times, ch 6, sk 2 sc*, 1 sc in next sc; rep from * to * once, join with a sl st to 1st sc (20 ch-6 lps).

RND 7: Ch 1, 1 sc in 1st sc, *(7 sc in next ch-6 lp, sk 1 sc, 1 sc in next sc) 9 times, 7 sc in next ch-6 lp*, 1 sc in next sc; rep from * to * once, join with a sl st to 1st sc.

RND 8 (INC RND): Ch 1, 1 sc in 1st sc, *ch 6, sk 2 sc, 1 sc in ea of next 3 sc, (ch 6, sk 5 sc, 1 sc in ea of next 3 sc) 9 times, ch 6, sk 2 sc*, 1 sc in next sc; rep from * to * once, join with a sl st to 1st sc (22 ch-6 lps).

RND 9: Ch 1, 1 sc in 1st sc, *(7 sc in next ch-6 lp, sk 1 sc, 1 sc in next sc) 10 times, 7 sc in next ch-6 lp*, 1 sc in next sc; rep from * to * once, join with a sl st to 1st sc.

■ **skill level**

Experienced

■ **finished measurements**

Approx 14 x 14"/36 x 36cm, not including handles

■ **you will need**

Approx 504yd/454m sport weight rayon yarn

Hook: 4.5mm/G-6 or size needed to obtain gauge

18 x 34"/45 x 86cm piece of lining fabric

Paper to create lining pattern

Scissors

Straight pins

Sewing needle and matching thread

Sewing machine (optional)

■ **stitches used**

Chain stitch (ch)

Single crochet (sc)

Slip stitch (sl st)

■ **gauge**

Take time to check your gauge.

6 arches = 6"/15cm

8 rows = 2"/5cm over pattern stitch

Ooh-La-La Tote

**RND 10
(INC RND):** Ch 1, 1 sc in 1st sc, *ch 6, sk 2 sc, 1 sc in ea of next 3 sc, (ch 6, sk 5 sc, 1 sc in ea of next 3 sc) 10 times, ch 6, sk 2 sc*, 1 sc in next sc; rep from * to * once, join with a sl st to 1st sc (24 ch-6 lps).

RND 11: Ch 1, 1 sc in 1st sc, *(7 sc in next ch-6 lp, sk 1 sc, 1 sc in next sc) 11 times, 7 sc in next ch-6 lp*, 1 sc in next sc; rep from * to * once, join with a sl st to 1st sc.

RND 12: Ch 1, 1 sc in 1st sc, *ch 3, sk 2 sc, 1 sc in ea of next 3 sc, (ch 6, sk 5 sc, 1 sc in ea of next 3 sc) 11 times, ch 3, sk 2 sc*, 1 sc in next sc, rep from * to * once, join with a sl st to 1st sc.

RND 13: Ch 1, 1 sc in 1st sc, *3 sc in next ch-3 lp, sk 1 sc, 1 sc in next sc, (7 sc in next ch-6 lp, sk 1 sc, 1 sc in next sc) 11 times, 3 sc in next ch-3 lp *, 1 sc in next sc; rep from * to *, join with a sl st to 1st sc.

RND 14: Ch 1, 1 sc in 1st sc, 1 sc in next sc, (ch 6, sk 5 sc, 1 sc in ea of next 3 sc) 23 times, ch 6, sk 5 sc, 1 sc in next sc, join with a sl st to 1st sc.

RND 15: Ch 1, 1 sc in 1st sc, (7 sc in next ch-6 lp, sk 1 sc, 1 sc in next sc) 23 times, 7 sc in next ch-6 lp, sk 1 sc, join with a sl st to 1st sc.

RND 16: Ch 1, 1 sc in 1st sc, *ch 3, sk 2 sc, 1 sc in ea of next 3 sc, (ch 6, sk 5 sc, 1 sc in ea of next 3 sc)11 times, ch 3, sk 2 sc, * 1 sc in next sc; rep from * to * once, join with a sl st to 1st sc.

RND 17: Ch 1, 1 sc in 1st sc, *3 sc in next ch-3 lp, sk 1 sc, 1 sc in next sc, (7 sc in next ch-6 lp, sk 1 sc, 1 sc in next sc) 11 times, 3 sc in next ch-3 lp *, 1 sc in next sc; rep from * to * once, join with a sl st to 1st sc.

RND 18 (INC RND): Ch 1, 1 sc in 1st sc, *ch 3, sk 1 sc, 1 sc in next sc, ch 6, sk 4 sc, 1 sc in ea of next 3 sc, (ch 6, sk 5 sc, 1 sc in ea of next 3 sc) 10 times, ch 6, sk 4 sc, 1 sc in next sc, ch 3, sk 1 sc *, 1 sc in next sc; rep from * to * once, join with a sl st to 1st sc. (24 ch-6 lps plus 4 ch-3 lps which will count as 2 ch-6 lps for a total of 26 ch-6 lps)

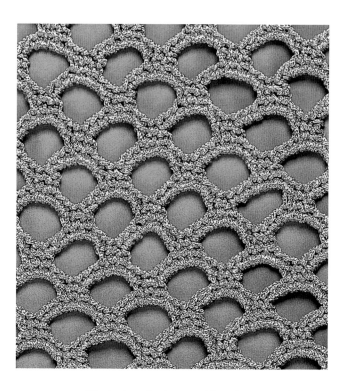

RND 19: Ch 1, 1 sc in 1st sc, *3 sc in next ch-3 lp, 1 sc in next sc, (7 sc in next ch-6 lp, sk 1 sc, 1 sc in next sc) 11 times, 7 sc in next ch-6 lp, 1 sc in next sc, 3 sc in next ch-3 lp *, 1 sc in next sc; rep from * to * once, join with a sl st to 1st sc.

RND 20: Ch 1, 1 sc in same sc, 1 sc in next sc, (ch 6, sk 5 sc, 1 sc in ea of next 3 sc) 25 times, ch 6, sk 5 sc, 1 sc in next sc, join with a sl st to 1st sc.

RND 21: Ch 1, 1 sc in same sc, (7 sc in next ch-6 lp, sk 1 sc, 1 sc in next sc) 25 times, 7 sc in next ch-6 lp, sk 1 sc, join with a sl st to 1st sc.

RND 22: Ch 6, *sk 2 sc, 1 sc in ea of next 3 sc, (ch 6, sk 5 sc, 1 sc in ea of next 3 sc) 12 times, ch 3*, sk 2 sc, 1 dc in next sc, ch 3; rep from * to * once, join with a sl st to 3rd ch of beg ch-6.

RND 23: Ch 1, 1 sc in same sc, *3 sc in next ch-3 lp, sk 1 sc, 1 sc in next sc, (7 sc in next ch-6 lp, sk 1 sc, 1 sc in next sc) 12 times, 3 sc in next ch-3 lp*, 1 sc in next dc; rep from * to * once, join with a sl st to 1st sc.

RND 24: Rep rnd 20.

RND 25: Rep rnd 21.

RND 26: Rep rnd 22.

RND 27: Rep rnd 23.

Continue to rep rnds 20–23 six more times until 51 rnds total.

Fasten off.

Tote Handles (make 2)

Ch 81.

ROW 1: Work 1 sc in 2nd ch from hk and in ea of next 79 ch, turn (80 sc).

ROW 2: Ch 1, 1 sc in ea sc, turn.

ROW 3: Ch 1, 1 sc in ea sc, turn.

ROW 4: Ch 1, 1 sc in ea sc.

Fasten off.

Finishing

Block bag by pinning it out on a flat surface and using a warm iron to steam. Do not touch the iron to the thread. Block the handles to flatten.

Lining

Place the blocked bag on paper and trace around outline to create the lining pattern. Cut out the pattern.

Fold the lining fabric in half (18 x 17"/46 x 43cm) with right sides (RS) facing. Pin paper pattern to lining fabric, aligning bottom edge of paper pattern to the folded fabric edge.

Cut lining fabric at least 1"/2.5cm beyond paper pattern to create seam allowance around the edge of the bag. Stitch sides of the lining together with a sewing machine or by hand, following along the side edges of the paper pattern. Trim excess fabric to ½"/1cm for seam allowance. Turn RS out and press seams and bottom fold well with an iron.

Fold lining over twice toward the wrong side (WS) of fabric. Pin in place so the raw cut edge of lining fabric is hidden. Slip lining into the bag. If needed, adjust lining hem to the height of the bag. Remove lining from bag and press to flatten. Stitch around top edge with a sewing machine or by hand to secure the folded hem.

Lay the bag flat and press the sides with your hands. Pin ea end of one handle to top edge of bag at the 3rd arch in from both edges. Overlap edge of bag approximately 1"/2.5cm over end of handle. Stitch handle loops in place by hand. Repeat with second handle. Slip lining into bag. Tack bottom corners of lining to bottom of bag. Hand stitch hemmed edge of lining to top edge of crocheted bag.

This project was created with
4 balls of Gedifra's *Crystal* in chartreuse (#2517), 100% nylon, 1.75oz/50g balls = approx 126yd/115m ea

Flirty Floral Choker

A simple crocheted band is edged with delicate picots and embellished with three simple posies (or more—the choice is yours). Start this one Saturday morning and show it off that evening.

DESIGN BY
Katherine Lee

Pattern Notes

Picot = Ch 3, sl st in 1st ch.

The pattern stitch in the band is worked over a multiple of 3 sts plus 5.

Band

Row 1: Ch 74, work 1 dc in 5th ch from hk, *ch 1, sk 1 ch, 1 dc in ea of next 2 ch; rep from * to end, do not turn.

Edging Round

Working counterclockwise around the 4 edges of row 1, ch 1, (2 sc, picot, 2 sc) in sp created by last dc of row 1, picot, 1 sc in base ch of last dc of row 1, 1 sc in base ch of next dc, picot, *skip 1 base ch, 1 sc in ea of next 2 base ch, picot; rep from * to base ch of 1st dc of row 1, 1 sc in base ch of 1st dc of row 1, (1 sc, picot, 2 sc, picot, 2 sc, picot, 1 sc) in sp created by ch-5 of row 1, 1 sc in next dc, picot, **1 sc in ea of next 2 dc, picot; rep from ** back to 1st corner, join with a sl st to 1st sc. Fasten off.

Flower Motifs (make 3)

RND 1: Wind yarn around finger to form small ring. Ch 1, 13 sc in ring, join with a sl st to 1st sc.

RND 2: (Ch 4, sk 1 sc, sl st into next sc) 6 times, ch 4, join with a sl st to 1st ch of ch 4 = 7 ch-4 lps.

RND 3: Ch 3, (6 dc, picot, 6 dc) in each ch-4 lp around, join with a sl st to 3rd ch of beg ch-3. Fasten off.

Finishing

Lightly steam band. Do not steam flowers. Sew flowers onto band as desired. Tack leaves of flowers to each other as needed. Sew snaps on band to fit neck comfortably, using 2 snaps for smaller neck sizes.

■ **skill level**

Intermediate

■ **finished measurements**

Approx 1 x 15"/2.5 x 38cm

■ **you will need**

100yd/91m sport weight silk yarn

Hook: 4.5mm/G-6 or size needed to obtain gauge

(1 or 2) #3 snaps

Sewing needle and matching thread

■ **stitches used**

Chain (ch)

Double crochet (dc)

Slip stitch (sl st)

■ **gauge**

Take time to check your gauge.

16 dc = 4"/10cm over pattern stitch for choker band

This project was created with

1 ball of Adrienne Vittadini's *Celia* in pink (#538),100% silk, 1oz/25g ball = approx 109yd/98m

Hipster Sash Belts

Wear one…or two…or even three.
How hip do you feel? It's up to you.

DESIGN BY
Marty Miller

Pattern Notes

You start working these belts in a row, then work around the row: first around the side, then the bottom, the other side, and ending on the top.

How to start the belt if you don't want to count your stitches: Make a loose chain that measures approximately as long you want the belt to be. Chain a few more—just in case.

Then, starting with row 1, follow the directions until you get near the end of the foundation chain. Measure the belt—if it's about as long as you want it, finish the first row by making a Bbl st in the pattern, ch1, skip next ch, dc in next ch, dc in next ch. Ch 1, do not turn. The extra foundation chains at the end of the row can be unknotted up to the last stitch when you are finished with the belt.

To make a belt shorter or longer, chain a multiple of 4 (56, 60, 64, 68) plus 2 additional ch for your foundation chain.

Narrow Belt

Foundation Chain: Leave a long tail (approx 8"/20cm), ch a multiple of 4, plus 2, to measure approx 65"/165cm.

ROW 1: Dc in 4th ch from hk. Ch 1, sk next ch in foundation, Bbl st in next ch. Ch 1, sk next ch in foundation, *dc in next ch, ch 1, sk next ch, Bbl st in next ch, ch 1, sk next ch. Rep from * across, ending dc in next ch, dc in last ch. Ch 1, do not turn.

Edging

RND 1: 3 sc around the post of the last dc in row 1. Sc in each bottom loop of the foundation chain, 3 sc around the 3 chs at the beg of row 1, sc in each dc, Bbl st, and ch-1 sp across the top. End with sl st in first sc. Fasten off, leaving an 8"/20cm tail.

Fringe

For each end of the belt, cut twenty 16"/41cm pieces of yarn. Fold in half and join all together at the ends of the belt, over the dc or ch-3 posts, including in the fringe the long tails of yarn you left at the beginning and the end.

■ **skill level**

Easy

■ **finished measurements**

Belt is approx 65"/1.7m long, without fringe.

■ **you will need**

Approx 120yd/108m worsted weight lavender or green yarn for a narrow belt

Approx 240yd/216m worsted weight orange yarn for a wide belt

Hook: 6.5mm/K/10½ or size needed to obtain gauge

■ **gauge**

Gauge isn't critical in this pattern.

■ **stitches used**

Chain stitch (ch)

Single crochet (sc)

Double crochet (dc)

Slip stitch (sl st)

Bobble Stitch (Bbl st)

Beg the Bbl st like a dc in the desired st. In other words, yo, put hk through st and draw up a loop, yo, pull through 2 lps. You have just made the post of the Bbl St.

*Yo hook and insert the hook from the front around the back and to the front of the post. Yo, pull up a loop around the post, rep from * 2 more times. Yo hook and draw through all 8 loops on hook to form the Bbl St.

Hipster Sash Belts

Wide Belt

Foundation Chain: Leaving a long tail approx 8"/20cm, ch a multiple of 4, plus 2, to measure approx 65"/165cm.

ROW 1: Dc in 4th ch from hook. Ch 1, sk next ch in foundation, Bbl st in next ch. Ch 1, sk next ch in foundation, *dc in next ch, ch 1, sk next ch, Bbl st in next ch, ch 1, sk next ch. Rep from * across, ending dc in next ch, dc in last ch. Ch 1, turn.

ROW 2: Sc in each st and ch-1 sp across. Ch 3 (counts as dc), turn.

ROW 3: Sk first sc, *dc in next sc, ch1, skip 1 sc, Bbl st in next sc, ch-1, skip next sc, rep from * across, ending dc in next ch, dc in last ch. Ch 1, do not turn.

Edging

ROUND 1: 2 sc around the post of the last dc in row 3, 2 sc around the post of the last dc in row 1, *sc in the next ch-1 sp, sc in the bottom lp of the same ch where there is a Bbl st, sc in the next ch-1 sp, sc in the bottom lp of the same ch where there is a dc, repeat from * across, ending sc in the bottom lp of the same ch where there is a dc, 2 sc around the ch 3 at the beginning of row 1, 2 sc around the ch 3 at the beg of row 3, sc in each dc, Bbl st, and ch-1 sp across. End with sl st in first sc. Fasten off, leaving an 8"/20cm tail.

This project was created with

1 skein of Berroco's *Suede* in Calamity Jane (#3745) or Tonto (#3715); 2 skeins of Clementine (#3757), 100% nylon, 1.75oz/50g = approx 120yd/108m per skein.

Fringe

For each end of the belt, cut twenty 16"/41cm pieces of yarn. Fold in half and join all together at the ends of the belt, over the dc or ch-3 posts, including in the fringe the long tails of yarn that you left at the beginning and the end.

Perfect Little Bag

Perfect for either evening or daytime—take your pick. This gem of a bag is worked in one simple stitch with a heavy cotton thread that's both durable and great to crochet with. Add specially selected decorative beads to the drawstring cord for a dressy look.

DESIGN BY
Barbara Zaretsky

Perfect Little Bag

■ skill level
Beginner

■ finished measurements
Approx 5 x 5"/13 x 13cm

■ you will need
Color A: Approx 108yd/97m heavy worsted weight mercerized cotton thread in green

Color B: Approx 108yd/97m heavy worsted weight mercerized cotton thread in beige

Hook: 5mm/H-8 or size needed to obtain gauge

Stitch marker

Tapestry needle

Decorative beads

■ stitches used
Chain st (ch)

Single crochet (sc)

■ gauge
Take time to check your gauge.
Approx 6 sc = 1"/2.5cm

Pattern Notes

This project is worked in a spiral. Turning chains are not needed at the end of a rnd.

Body

Ch 8 and join with sl st.

RND 1: 2 sc in each ch, mark end of rnd (16 st).

RND 2: * Sc in first st, 2 sc in next st, rep from * to end of rnd. Mark end of rnd.

RND 3: *Sc in next 2 sts and 2 sc in 3rd st, rep from * to end of rnd. Mark end of rnd.

RND 4: *Sc in next 3 sts and 2 sc in the 4th st, rep from * to end of rnd. Mark end of rnd.

RND 5: *Sc in next 4 sts and 2 sc in the 5th st, rep from * to end of rnd. Mark end of rnd.

RND 6: *Sc in next 5 sts and 2 sc in the 6th st, rep from * to end of rnd. Mark end of rnd.

RND 7: *Sc in next 6 sts and 2 sc in the 7th st, rep from * to end of rnd. Mark end of rnd.

RND 8: *Sc in next 7 sts and 2 sc in the 8th st, rep from * to end of rnd. Mark end of rnd.

RND 9: Change to color B, *sc in next 8 sts and 2 sc in the 9th st, rep from * to end of rnd. Mark end of rnd.

RND 10: Change to color A, *sc in next 9 sts and 2 sc in the 10th st, rep from * to end of rnd. Mark end of rnd.

RNDS 11–32: Sc in ea st. Mark end of each rnd.

Change to color B for stripe on rows: 13, 17, 21, 25 and 29 or as desired.

Edging

RND 33: From end of row 32, *ch 4, sk 3 sc, sc in next st, rep from * around the row. Mark end of rnd.

RND 34: *Sc in first 4 st, sk next st* rep from * to finish rnd. Mark.

RND 35: Sc in each st. Mark end.

RND 36: *Sc in first st and 2 sc in next st, rep from * to finish row. Fasten off.

Turn bag inside out and weave in thread ends.

Drawstring Cord

Work with 2 strands ea approx 4yd/4m long. Ch st until strand is approx 1yd/1m long.

Trim end to 3"/8cm and pull yarn through last st to fasten off.

Knot end of chain, add bead and knot again

Lace crocheted cord through holes. Knot cord approx 4"/10cm from end.

This project was created with

1 skein each of Tahki's *Cotton Classic* in green (3763) and linen (3200), 100% mercerized cotton, 1.75oz/50g = approx 108yd/97m per skein

On the Double Cloche

This simply chic little cap is a perfect introduction to working in the round. Experienced crocheters can whip up several… on the double.

DESIGN BY
Kalpna Kapoor

■ **skill level**
Beginner

■ **finished measurements**
The finished cloche will fit most adults.

■ **you will need**
Approx 165yd/149m ribbon yarn
Hook: 6.5mm/K-10½ or size needed to obtain gauge

■ **stitches used**
Chain stitch (ch)
Double crochet (dc)
Slip stitch (sl st)

■ **gauge**
Take time to check your gauge.
13 sts and 7 rows = 4"/10cm in dc

This project was created with
2 balls of Lana Grossa's *Doppio* in tan (#11), 56% cotton/44% nylon, 1.75 oz/50g = approx 82 yd/74m

Pattern Note
This cloche is worked from the top down.

Pattern
Ch 5, sl st in 1st ch to form ring.

RND 1: Ch 3 (counts as dc), work 11 dc in ring. Join with sl st in top of ch 3 (12 dc).

RND 2: Ch 3 (counts as dc), 1 dc in same st as join, 2 dc in each dc around. Join with a sl st in top of ch 3 (24 dc).

RND 3: Ch 3 (counts as dc), 1 dc in same st as join, *1 dc in next st, 2 dc in next st; rep from * to last st, 1 dc in last st. Join with a sl st in top of ch 3 (36 dc).

RND 4: Ch 3 (counts as dc), 1 dc in same st as join, *1 dc in next 2 sts, 2 dc in next st; rep from * to last 2 st, 2 dc in each of last 2 sts. Join with a sl st in top of ch 3 (50 dc).

RND 5: Ch 3 (counts as dc), 1 dc in same st as join, *1 dc in next 3 sts, 2 dc in next st; rep from * to last 3 st, 3 dc in each of last 2 sts. Join with a sl st in top of ch 3 (67 dc).

Discontinue incs and cont even in dc in rnds. (Working in even rnds will give the hat a bowl shape.) Work even until hat measures desired length from center of crown.

NEXT 4 RNDS: Sc in each st around and fasten off.

Weave in all yarn ends.

Urban Beach Tote

This tote is just as at home when you're trudging down city streets as it is when you're strolling on tropical white sands or down country lanes.

DESIGN BY
Lindsay Obermeyer

- **skill level**

  Intermediatev

- **finished measurements**

  Approx 12 x 16 x 4½"/30 x 41 x 11cm

- **you will need**

  Approx 810yd/729m sport weight linen or cotton yarn in green

  Approx 270yd/243m sport weight linen or cotton yarn in off-white

  Hook: 3.25mm/D-3 or size needed to obtain gauge

  4 buttons

  Tapestry needle

- **stitches used**

  Chain stitch (ch)

  Single crochet (sc)

  Half double crochet (hdc)

- **gauge**

  Take time to check your gauge.

  5 sc and 4 rows = 1"/2.5cm

Tote Bottom

Using the green yarn, ch 82.

Sc in 2nd chain from hk and in each remaining ch until end. *Chain 1. Turn work and sc into 2nd ch from hk with hk inserted into both halves of the st. Cont until end of row.* Repeat procedure from * to * until bottom is approx 4½"/11cm wide.

Tote Body

Work in rounds.

Make 26 hdc evenly along short side into back loop (BL) of stes until you come to the first corner. Work 3 hdc into corner st. Turn and hdc along the long side into BL of st until you come to 2nd corner. Work 3 hdc into corner st. Turn and make 26 hdc evenly along short side into BL of stes until you come to 3rd corner. Work 3 hdc into corner st. Turn and hdc along the long side into BL of st until you come to the final corner. Work 3 hdc into corner st.

Work hdc around, into both halves of the st until height of tote measures approx 12"/30 cm. Finish off with sl st, cut yarn, and fasten off. Weave in all ends.

Picot Edging

Using off-white yarn, fasten the yarn to the 1st st. *Ch 3, 1 sc in the first of the ch-3 sts. Sk 1 st on the crochet work. 1 sc in the next st. Rep from * around. Finish picot edge with sl st in first st. Cut yarn and fasten off. Weave in the end.

Handles (make 2)

Using off-white yarn, ch 13. Work in rows, in sc in both halves of the st for approx 2½"/6cm. Connect using a sl st. Working in rnds, sc in both halves of the st for approx 16"/41cm. The front side does not show the opening to the tube, so with front side facing you sc across 7 st , ch 1. Turn and insert hk into 2nd st from hk, sc across 8 st , ch 1. Turn and insert hk into 2nd st from hk, sc across 9 st and increase 1, ch 1. Turn and insert hk into 2nd st from hk, sc across 10 st , ch 1 (11 sc).

Continue working in rows with sc in both halves of the st until approx 2½"/6cm long, do not chain on last row, when sc in final st, cut yarn and fasten off.

Repeat to make another handle, weave in all ends.

Finishing

With the bag laying flat, measure in from each side 4"/10cm and line up outer edge of handle tabs. Pin with top edge of tab before increase/decrease to top row of hdc on bag. Using green yarn, st handles to bag with a running stitch using tapestry needle. Knot and weave in ends. Sew buttons to handle tabs to finish.

This project was created with

3 skeins Euroflax's *Linen Yarn* in willow (18-2554) and 1 skein Euroflax's *Linen Yarn* in natural (18-2304), each 3.5oz/100g = approx 270yd/243m per skein

Spiral design water buffalo horn buttons (NPL 340-31B) from One World Button Supply Company

Paisley Motif Scarf

The lush colors and *boteh* motifs of this soft scarf echo the tones and patterns found on finely woven Paisley shawls, yet are playful and modern.

DESIGN BY
Donna May

■ **skill level**
Easy

■ **finished measurements**
Scarf body approx 8 x 35"/20 x 76cm (before motifs are attached)

Paisleys approx 3½ x 2½"/8 x 5cm

■ **you will need**
For scarf body: approx 328yd/295m multicolor bulky weight yarn

For boteh motifs: approx 540 yd/486m fingering weight yarn in red (A), orange (B), and dark brown (C)

Hooks: 10mm/N-15 and 4mm/G-6 or sizes needed to obtain gauge

Tapestry needle

■ **stitches used**
Chain stitch (ch)
Half double crochet (hdc)
Double crochet (dc)
Single crochet (sc)

■ **gauge**
Take time to check your gauge.
Approx 10 stitches = 4"/10cm with 10mm/N-15 hook

Scarf Body

Using 10mm/N-15 hook and bulky weight yarn, ch 21.

ROW 1: Sc in 2nd st and ea st across; ch 1, turn (20 sts). Tie a contrasting color yarn around a st in 1st row to mark RS.

ROWS 2–98 (OR UNTIL SCARF REACHES DESIRED LENGTH): Sc in 1st st and each st across, turn, ch 1. Fasten off and weave in ends.

Boteh Motifs

Using 4mm/G-6 hook and fingering yarn, make 12 motifs (6 pairs).

Make 4 motifs with center color A. Of those, 2 with 2nd rnd color B, 3rd rnd color C, and 2 with 2nd rnd color C and 3rd rnd color B.

Make 4 motifs with center color B, and of those, 2 with 2nd rnd color A, 3rd rnd color C and 2 with 2nd rnd color C and 3rd rnd color A.

Make 4 motifs with center color C, and of those, 2 with 2nd rnd color A, 3rd rnd color B and 2 with 2nd rnd B and 3rd rnd C.

RND 1: With 4mm/G-6 hook, ch 12 and make 3 dc in 3rd ch from hk; 1 dc in next st; 1 hdc in each of next 2 sts; 1 dec sc in next st; 1 sc in ea of next 3 sts; 3 sc all in last st. Going around the corner and working under lps of foundation chain, 1 sc in first lp; 1 inc hdc in each of next 3 lps; 1 dc in next lp; 1 inc dc in ea of last 4 lps. Join with sl st in top of ch 3. Fasten off.

RND 2: Attach 2nd color yarn in st left of sl st and ch 3; (3dc in next st), twice; 1 hdc in next st; 1 sc in each of next 7 sts; 1 hdc and 1 sc both in next st; 1 sc in ea of next 7 sts; 1 hdc in next st; 1 inc dc in ea of next 3 sts; 1 dc in next st; (3 dc in next st), twice; 1 dc in next st. Join with sl st in top ch of ch 3. Fasten off.

Paisley Motif Scarf

This project was created with

4 balls of Berroco's *Monet* in Cherokee (# 9815), cotton/rayon/acrylic/nylon blend multicolor slub yarn, 1.75oz/49g = approx 82yd/74m ea

3 balls of Dalegarn's *Baby Ull* in Tomato Red (#3718), Orange (#2908), and Chocolate (#3364), 100% wool, 1.75oz/50g = approx 180yd/162m ea

RND 3: Attach 3rd color yarn in st left of sl st and ch 1; (3 sc in next st), 4 times; 1 sc in next st, 7 times; 1 sc and 1 hdc in next st; (3 sc in next st), 11 times; sc. Join with sl st in ch-1. Fasten off.

Weave in all ends.

Finishing

Lay scarf body flat, right side up. Divide the pairs of paisley motifs and place six of each color combination right side up on each end of scarf body. Arrange as desired.

When you have the motifs arranged as you like, thread tapestry needle with yarn and baste motifs to one end with running stitch. Repeat on opposite end. Fasten ends of yarn well, to insure the basting holds, as you'll be turning the piece many times while joining motifs.

Using G hook, join motifs to one another and to scarf ends with slip stitches in back loops of motifs or stitch them to the scarf with matching yarn.

Blocking isn't necessary. However, if you would like your motifs to lay flatter, place heavy books on the scarf ends overnight

Remove basting stitches. Weave in all ends.

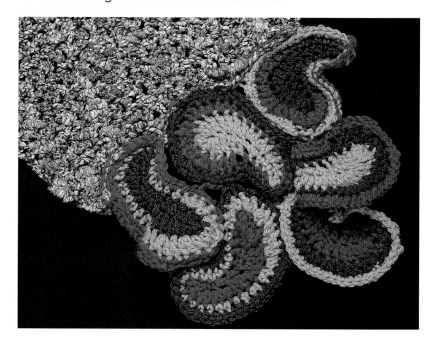

Bonny Fringed Poncho

Crochet two rectangles (using just one stitch) with an easy to work with cotton blend yarn, weave in a supple, variegated ribbon fringe, and join the two pieces. What could be simpler?

DESIGN BY
Gwen Blakley Kinsler

Bonny Fringed Poncho

■ **skill level**

Intermediate

■ **finished measurements**

Each rectangle approx 18 x 28"/46 x 71cm

■ **you will need**

850yd/765m of worsted weight cotton blend yarn

10yd/9m worsted weight cotton blend ribbon

Hook: 5mm/H-8 or size needed to obtain gauge

Tapestry needle

■ **stitches used**

Chain stitch (ch)

Double crochet (dc)

■ **gauge**

Take time to check your gauge.

4 dc = 1"/2.5cm

2 rows = 1"/2.5cm

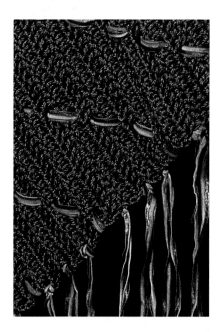

Pattern Notes

Chain 2 to turn each row. There are 13 dc between the ch-1 spaces. On each row, the ch-1 spaces move one space to create a diagonal row of spaces into which the ribbon will be woven. The stitches tend to pull up after several rows and the rectangle becomes slightly shorter.

Rectangle A

Ch 106 (approx 28"/71cm).

ROW 1: Dc in 6th ch from hk and in next 12 ch, *ch 1, sk 1 ch, dc in next 13 ch; rep from * 5 times, ch 1, sk 1 ch, dc in last 3 dc, turn.

ROW 2: Ch 2 (counts as dc), dc in next 2 dc, dc in space, dc in next dc, *ch 1, skip 1 dc, dc in next 13 dc, rep from * across (pattern), end 13 dc, turn.

Cont to follow chart (figure 1) from row 3 until piece measures approx 18"/46cm. Fasten off. Weave in ends.

Rectangle B

Ch 122 (approx 30"/76cm).

ROW 1: Dc in 6th ch from hk and in next 12 ch, *ch 1, sk 1 ch, dc in next 13 ch; rep from * 5 times, ch 1, skip 1 ch, dc in last 3 dc, turn.

ROW 2: Ch 2 (counts as dc), dc in next 2 dc, dc in space, dc in next dc, *ch 1, sk 1 dc, dc in next 13 dc, rep from * across (pattern), end 13 dc, turn.

Cont to follow chart from row 3 until piece measures approx 17"/43cm. Fasten off. Weave in ends.

Finishing

Measure the length of 1 diagonal row of spaces. Double the measurement and add 12"/31cm. Fold the ribbon in half. On the long edge of a rectangle, catch the outer edge of the fabric with the fold of the ribbon. Weave the ribbon ends as one through the diagonal row of spaces. The ribbon ends will hang on the waist side of the poncho. Knot the ribbon.

Measure and cut ribbon to weave the remaining diagonals one at a time.

If you'd prefer a denser fringed edge, add fringe between the woven ribbon ends. Measure and cut 16"/41cm lengths of ribbon. Fold one strand in half, bring your hook through the edge of the rectangle, and pull the folded end of the ribbon through the fabric. Insert your hook in the formed loop and pull the ends of the fringe through the loop and down to tighten.

Trim the ends of the fringe evenly.

Lay rectangles on a flat surface right side down with end and side butted up against each other. Join the end of Rectangle B to the side of Rectangle A. Cut 18"/46cm of worsted weight yarn. Thread the tapestry needle with the yarn and join to back of poncho. Insert needle first on left side of join, then right side for an invisible join (see page 000), taking care not to catch ribbon fringe.

Join the end of rectangle B to the side of rectangle A as described above. When the poncho is assembled, knot and weave in ends.

Add one 15"/38 cm length of ribbon fringe to center front of neck opening.

This project was created with

10 skeins of Berroco's *Cotton Twist* in Soul (#8387), 70% cotton/30% rayon, 1.75oz/50g = approx 85yd/78m ea

1 ball of Berroco's *Zen Ribbon* in Haruki (#8113), 55% cotton/45% nylon, 1.75oz/50g = approx 110yd/99m

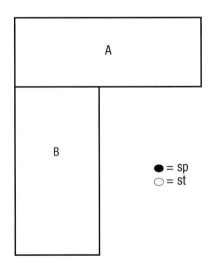

● = sp
○ = st

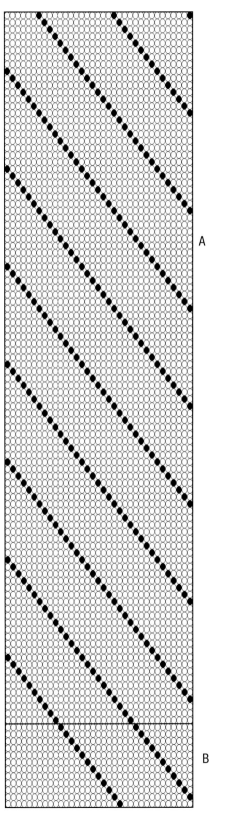

Side

A

B

Look What I Did With My Fingers!

DESIGN BY
Ruthie Marks

Feeling adventurous? Your friends may not believe you when you tell them how you made this sporty ensemble. Working with a bulky yarn makes this project a quick one—whether you choose to experiment with finger crochet or succumb to using a hook.

Pattern Notes

This project was created using finger crochet (see page 000). If you choose not to finger crochet, work the project with a 19mm/S hook.

Yarn A and yarn B are held together as one while working this project.

Do not join single crochet rounds unless instructed to join them.

Cut yarn for fringe and top knot before you begin:
16 strands of yarn B, each measuring 12"/30cm for the hat.
48 strands of yarn B, each measuring 15"/38cm for scarf

Make the hat first; then, with the remaining yarn, make the scarf to the desired length.

Hat

RND 1: Make a slipknot and, with your index finger, ch 3, 8 dc in 3rd ch from finger/hk, sl st to top of beg ch3 (9 sts).

RND 2: Ch 3, dc in same st, 2 dc in ea st around, sl st to top of beg ch 3 (18 sts).

RND 3: Ch 1, sc in ea sc around.

RNDS 4–11: Sc in ea sc around. At the end of rnd 11, sl st to first sc, fasten off, turn.

RND 12 (WS): Attach 2 strands of B with 1 sc and reverse sc in each st around, sl st to beg sc, fasten off.

Top Knot

Knot 1 folded end of strands and stuff knotted end through top of hat to wrong side. On the outside, tug free ends to make a snug connection. Trim evenly.

Scarf

ROW 1: Make a slipknot and, with your index finger, ch 7, sc in 2nd ch from finger/hk and next 3 ch, turn (6 st).

ROW 2: Ch 3 (counts as dc and first st), dc in next 5 sts, turn.

ROW 3: Ch 1, sc in ea st across, ending last sc in top of tch, turn.

Rep rows 2–3 until yarn is used up or to desired length, fasten off.

Fringe

Group 4 strands of fringe together and attach along short ends of scarf (see page 000). Trim evenly.

■ **skill level**
   Easy

■ **finished measurements**
   Hat: Fits most adults

   Scarf: approx 6 x 60"/15cm x 1.5m (excluding fringe)

■ **you will need**
   Yarn A: approx 156yd/140m bulky weight yarn

   Yarn B: approx 186yd/167m novelty yarn

   Hooks: 19mm/S (optional), use a smaller hook for attaching the fringe

   Tapestry needle

   Tapestry needle

■ **stitches used**
   Chain stitch (ch)

   Single crochet (sc)

   Double crochet (dc)

   Reverse single crochet (reverse sc)

   Half double crochet (hdc)

■ **gauge**
   Take time to check your gauge.

   2 st = 2"/5cm

   1 dc row and 1 sc row = 2½"/6cm

This project was created with

2 skeins Patons' *Upcountry* in Camel (#80912-B), 100% wool, 3.5 oz/98g = approx 78yd/70m ea

2 skeins Knit One Crochet Too *Jam* in Papaya (#821), 100% nylon, 1.75 oz/50g = approx 93yd84m ea

Mile Long Scarf

Well, truth be told, it's not really a mile long. But it's so much fun to make and wear that you'll be tempted to try it!

DESIGN BY
Robyn Kelley

■ skill level
Easy

■ finished measurements
Approx 5 x 91"/13cm x 2.3m

■ you will need
Yarn A: 154yd/139m blue super bulky eyelash yarn

Yarn B: 408yd/367m green light yarn

Hook: 6.5mm/K-10½ or size needed to obtain gauge

Yarn needle

■ stitches used
Chain stitch (ch)

Half double crochet (hdc)

Double crochet (dc)

■ gauge
Take time to check your gauge.

2 stitches and 8 rows = 3"/8cm

This project was created with

Yarn A: 2 balls Bernat's *Eye Lash* in Hip (#35142), 100% nylon, 1.75oz/50g = approx 77yd/70m ea

Yarn B: 3 balls Patons' *Grace* in Ginger (#60027). 100% mercerized cotton, 1.75oz/50g = approx 136yd/125m ea

Pattern Note
Color B is to be worked in back loops (BL) only of previous row.

Pattern

Using yarn A, ch 20.

ROW 1: 1 dc in 3rd ch from hook, 1 dc in ea ch across, ch 2, turn.

ROW 2: 1 dc in next dc and ea dc across, at last dc change to color B, ch 1, turn. Fasten off color A.

ROW 3: 1 sc in next dc and ea dc across, ch 1, turn.

ROW 4: 1 sc in BL only of next sc and ea sc across, ch 2, turn.

ROW 5: 1 hdc in BL only of next sc and ea sc across, ch 2, turn.

ROW 6: 1 hdc in BL only of next hdc and ea hdc across, ch 1, turn.

ROW 7–8: Rep rows 3–4. Remember to work in back lps.

ROW 9–10: Rep rows 5–6.

ROW 11–12: Rep rows 3–4.

ROW 13–14: Rep rows 5–6.

ROW 15–16: Rep rows 3–4, in last sc of Row 16 change to yarn A, ch 2, turn. Fasten off color B.

ROW 17: Using color A and working in both top lps now, 1 dc in next sc and ea sc across, ch 1, turn.

ROW 18: 1 dc in next dc and ea dc across, in last dc change to yarn B, ch 1, turn. Fasten off yarn A.

Continue repeating rows 3–18 until scarf measures approx. 91"/2.3m or desired length. You should end the scarf with the same color you started with. Weave in ends.

Oodles of Poodles Scarf

The combination of soft, black fuzzy yarn and variegated pinks evokes a vision of a 1950's poodle skirt, but with a contemporary twist.

DESIGN BY
Kalpna Kapoor

Pattern

With yarn A, ch 12.

ROW 1: Dc in 3rd ch from hook and in ea ch across row (10 dc), turn.

ROW 2: Ch 2, dc in 1st dc and each dc across; turn.

Rep row 2 until work measures approx 16"/41cm from beg. Cut yarn and fasten off.

Next row: Join yarn B, ch 2, dc in 1st dc and ea dc across; turn.

Rep row 2 until scarf measures approx 54"/137cm from beg. Cut yarn and fasten off.

Next row: Join yarn A, ch 2, dc in 1st dc and each dc across; turn.

Rep row 2 until scarf measures approx 70"/178cm from beg. Fasten off. Weave in all thread ends.

Fringe

Cut lengths of yarns A and B measuring approx 8"/20cm long. Holding 2 strands of A and 2 strands of B together, knot into fringe on lower edge of scarf on both sides (see page 000) .

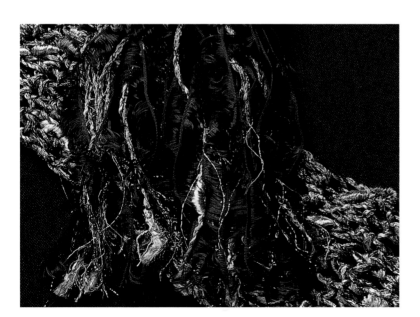

■ **skill level**

Beginner

■ **finished measurements**

Approx 3 x 80"/8 x 203cm long (excluding fringes)

■ **you will need**

Color A: approx 124yd/112m pink heavy worsted yarn

Color B: approx 71yd/64m black bulky yarn
Hook: 8mm/L-11

■ **stitches used**

Chain stitch (ch)

Double crochet (dc)

■ **gauge**

Gauge is not crucial for this pattern.

This project was created with

2 balls of Muench Yarn's *Cleo* (#181), 87% viscose/13% metal, 1.75oz/50g = approx 62yd/56m ea

1 ball of Bernat's *Boa* in Raven (#81040), 100% polyester, 1.75oz/50g = approx 71yd/65m

Orange Sorbet Wrap

A wrap as light and refreshing as…you guessed it! If you've been leery of working with fancy novelty yarns, this simple shawl in an open lace stitch pattern is a great project—especially suitable for a beginner. You won't run into the difficulty of inserting your hook in hard-to-locate stitch loops: you work your double crochets into a space instead.

DESIGN BY
Katherine Lee

■ **skill level**

Beginner

■ **finished measurements**

Approx 57 x 27"/145 x 68cm (excluding fringe)

■ **you will need**

Approx 330yd/297m of ⅜"/10mm wide ribbon yarn

Hook: 11.5mm/P-16 or size needed to obtain gauge

■ **stitches used**

Chain stitch (ch)

Slip stitch (sl st)

Double crochet (dc)

■ **gauge**

Take time to check your gauge.

4 sets of (1 dc, ch 1) and 4 rows = 4"/10cm over pattern stitch

This project was created with

5 balls of GGH's *Celine* ribbon yarn in Orange Cream (#12), 35% cotton/65% nylon, 1oz/50g = approx 66yd/60m ea

Pattern

Begin work at the bottom point of the triangle.

Ch 4, join with a sl st to 1st ch to form ring.

ROW 1: Ch 4 (counts as 1 dc, ch 1), 1 dc in ring, (ch 1, 1 dc in ring) 2 times, turn.

ROW 2: Ch 4 (counts as 1 dc, ch 1), 1 dc in 1st dc, ch 1, (1 dc in next ch-1 sp, ch 1) 2 times, (1 dc, ch 1, 1 dc) in ch-4 sp created by tch, turn.

ROW 3: Ch 4 (counts as 1 dc, ch 1), 1 dc in 1st dc, ch 1, *1 dc in next ch-1 sp, ch 1; rep from * to tch, (1 dc, ch 1, 1 dc) in ch-4 sp created by tch, turn.

Rep row 3 until you have 28 rows total. Fasten off.

Finishing

Cut 17"/43cm lengths of yarn. Using 1 folded strand for each fringe, place fringe evenly at each ch-4 sp and dc along bottom edges and at ch-4 ring at bottom corner (see page 29).

Flip Scarf

The fringe is so delightful you may not be able to prevent your hands from fiddling with it. The trick to the spiralling fringe is simple: It's only double crochet!

DESIGN BY
Lindsay Obermeyer

■ skill level
Easy

■ finished measurements
Approx 8 x 62"/20cm x 1.6m (excluding trim or fringe)

■ you will need
Approx 680yd/612m fingering weight wool

Hook: 3.75mm/F-5

Tapestry needle

■ stitches used
Chain stitch (ch)

Double crochet (dc)

Single crochet (sc)

Half double crochet (hdc)

■ gauge
Take time to check your gauge.

6 dc and 3 rows =1"/2.5cm

This project was created with

4 skeins of Koigu's *Handpainted KPM* (#P612), 100% Merino wool, 1.75oz/50g = approx 170yd/153m ea

Scarf Body

Ch 44 sts. *Insert hk into 2nd st from hk and dc into each st until end. Ch 1, turn.* Rep from *to * until you reach desired length.

On the last row ch 1 and turn work.

Fringe (worked on short edges of scarf)

You will work an edge of fringe, followed by scallop edging, then repeat an edge of fringe and edging around the scarf.

Insert hk into 2nd st from hk and sc into the st to begin corkscrew fringe. *Ch 45 st. Turn , 1 dc into the 3rd stitch from the hook. Continue with 3 dc in each ch st up to the last 5 ch sts, then 1 hdc, 1 dc, 3 sl st and 4 dc in the edge of the crochet work.* Rep across short edge of scarf from * to *. Finish row with 1 sc.

Scallop Edging (on long edge of scarf)

You have just finished with an sc. Ch 1, insert hk into first st of long edge, and sc. *Sk 1 st. 5 dc into following st. Sk 1 st and sc.* Rep from * to *. You will notice that edge will ruffle a bit as the scallop edging is 2 sts shorter than typical to keep work flat. Once you have finished your last sc, ch 1. Insert hk into first st of 2nd short edge, sc.

When finished with 2nd series of corkscrews, return to scallop edging. Finish 2nd long edge of scarf with sc, cut yarn and fasten off. Sew in all ends with tapestry needle.

Lightly block scarf as needed.

Lacey Rainbow Scarf

DESIGN BY
Katherine Lee

This scarf is a perfect introduction to using pattern stitches. It's so easy that soon you'll be crocheting away, just enjoying the silky softness and glorious handpainted colors of the yarn as you go.

Special Pattern Stitch

Lace Stitch (worked over a multiple of 6 stitches plus 5)

ROW 1: 1 dc in 6th ch from hk, 1 dc in each of next 2 ch, ch 3, 1 dc in next ch, *sk 2 ch, 1 dc in ea of next 3 ch, ch 3, 1 dc in next ch; rep from * to last 2 ch, sk 1 ch, 1 dc in last ch, turn.

ROW 2: Ch 3 (counts as 1 dc), *(3 dc, ch 3, 1 dc) in next ch-3 sp; rep from * to last 3 dc, sk 3 dc, 1 dc in next ch, turn.

ROW 3: Ch 3 (counts as 1 dc), *(3 dc, ch 3, 1 dc) in next ch-3 sp; rep from * to last 4 dc, sk 3 dc, 1 dc in 3rd ch of t-ch, turn.

Rep row 3 for pattern.

Scarf

Ch 35, turn.

Work in Lace Stitch for rows 1–3.

Rep row 3 until scarf measures approx 80"/203cm (129 rows total). Fasten off.

Finishing

Lightly steam scarf and block as needed.

Cut 16"/41cm lengths of yarn (you will need 72). Using 3 strands for each fringe, attach 12 fringe ends evenly along each end of scarf (see page 000).

- **skill level**
  Beginner

- **finished measurements**
  Approx 6 x 80"/15 x 203cm (without fringe)

- **you will need**
  654yd/587m DK or light worsted weight wool/silk yarn

  Hook: 5mm/H-8 or size needed to obtain gauge

  Tapestry needle

- **stitches used**
  Chain stitch (ch)

  Double crochet (dc)

- **gauge**
  Take time to check your gauge.

  5 groups of (3 dc, ch 3, 1 dc) = 6"/15cm

  8 rows = 5"/13cm over lace stitch

This project was created with

3 hanks Schaefer's *Helene* in Isadora Duncan, 50% Merino wool/50% cultivated silk, 3oz/84g = approx 218yd/196m ea

Mermaid's Wrap

Glistening tones of sea greens and blues are the siren's call for this lightweight, asymmetrical wrap.

DESIGN BY
Jennifer Hansen

■ **skill level**

Intermediate

■ **finished measurements**

One size fits most. Approx 15 x 54"/38 x 137cm (before folding and excluding fringe)

■ **you will need**

Yarn A: approx 328yd/295m nylon or nylon blend worsted weight metallic yarn in variegated blue

Yarn B: approx 348yd/313m thick and thin glitter boucle yarn

Yarn C: approx 330yd/297m ribbon yarn

Hook: Tunisian Q hook or modified 16mm/Q or size needed to obtain gauge

Tapestry needle

■ **stitches used**

Chain stitch (ch)

Slip stitch (sl st)

Tunisian simple stitch (Tss) (page 20)

Tunisian slip stitch (Tsl) (page 21)

■ **gauge**

Take time to check your gauge.

Approx 10 sts = 4" in Tss/Tsl Pattern Stitch

Pattern Notes

A colorful, woven tapestry effect is deceptively simple to achieve. Working with three different colors, you use a simple color change of yarn at the beginning and end of each row. You pick up the yarn left there from the previous row.

This technique relies on a simple, repeated pattern of Tunisian simple stitch (Tss) followed by Tunisian slip stitch (Tsl). Ending edge stitches are always worked in Tss.

Typically, Tunisian (Afghan) crochet requires a special hook (see page 20). Because this poncho is not very wide and will require relatively few stitches, you may choose to use a standard Q hook. If desired, you may modify a Q hook by cutting out a 1"/2.5cm circle of cardboard and slipping it onto your hook. Secure the circle to the end of the hook by wrapping a rubber band tightly over the end.

Tunisian Crochet Tip: When working Tunisian crochet, the outside stitch of the starting edge of the work tends to become very loose because it's the stitch that remains on the hook the longest, and the action of the hook works to loosen it. In order to counteract this tendency, work the first stitch of the row in the BACK vertical bar of the stitch in order to achieve a tidy fabric edge.

Tunisian Crochet Tip: Periodically check the number of loops on your hook as you work.

Color Change

You'll change the color at the beginning of every reverse and forward pass when creating this poncho. In order to create a fabric with a consistent, neat edge, follow these guidelines when changing color.

BEGINNING OF FORWARD PASS: Change colors when 2 loops remain on the hook from the preceding Reverse pass. Yarn over with new color, and pull through the last 2 loops on the hk. You now have one loop on the hook—this loop is the first stitch of the forward pass. Work the forward pass in the new yarn.

BEGINNING OF REVERSE PASS: At the end of the forward pass work the last stitch as usual. Before picking up with the new color yarn, grab the tail of yarn worked in the forward pass and bring it over the hook from the front. Start the first stitch of the reverse pass with the new yarn, pulling a loop of the new color yarn under the 2 strands of the previous yarn.

Mermaid's Wrap

Ch 41 with yarn A, turn.

ROW 1: Work a standard Tunisian base row (41 lps on hk). For reverse pass, drop A to side of work; do not cut. Work lps off hk with B until 2 lps rem on hk. Drop B to side of work, do not cut. With C, yo, pull through 2 lps on hk.

ROW 2: Continuing with C, sk 1st st. [Tss in next st (back vertical bar for first worked st), Tsl in following st] across until last 2 sts. Tss in next st, tss in edge st. For reverse pass, drop C to side of work; do not cut. Work loops off hk with A until 2 lps rem on hk. Drop A to side of work, do not cut. With B, yo, pull through 2 lps on hk.

ROW 3: Continuing with B, sk first st. [Tsl in next st, Tss in following st] across until last 2 sts. Tsl in next st, tss in edge st. For reverse pass, drop B to side of work; do not cut. Work loops off hk with C until 2 lps rem on hk. Drop C to side of work, do not cut. With A, yo, pull through 2 lps on hk.

ROW 4: Continuing with A, sk 1st st. [Tss in next st (back vertical bar for first worked st), Tsl in following st] across until last 2 sts. Tss in next st, tss in edge st. For reverse pass, drop A to side of work; do not cut. Work loops off hk with B until 2 lps rem on hk. Drop B to side of work, do not cut. With C, yo, pull through 2 lps on hk.

ROW 5: Continuing with C, sk 1st st. [Tsl in next st, Tss in following st] across until last 2 sts. Tsl in next st, tss in edge st. For reverse pass, drop C to side of work; do not cut. Work loops off hk with A until 2 lps rem on hk. Drop A to side of work, do not cut. With B, yo, pull through 2 lps on hk.

ROW 6: Continuing with B, sk 1st st. [Tss in next st (back vertical bar for first worked st), Tsl in following st] across until last 2 sts. Tss in next st, Tss in edge st. For reverse pass, drop B to side of work; do not cut. Work loops off hk with C until 2 lps rem on hk. Drop C to side of work, do not cut. With A, yo, pull through 2 lps on hk.

ROW 7: Continuing with A, sk first st. [Tsl in next st, Tss in following st] across until last 2 sts. Tsl in next st, Tss in edge st. For reverse pass, drop A to side of work; do not cut. Work loops off hk with B until 2 lps rem on hk. Drop B to side of work, do not cut. With C, yo, pull through 2 lps on hk.

REMAINING ROWS: Work as for rows 2–7 in repeating sequence until work measures approx 54"/137cm long.

LAST ROW: (Bind Off/Forward Pass only) With next color in sequence, sk first st. Sl st in each vertical bar across. Tie off, leaving long tail, approx 45"/114cm for seaming.

Finishing

Weave in ends on WS of fabric. If fabric is uneven, lightly block before seaming.

Fold rectangle in half as indicated in diagram (figure 1). Use yarn tail to seam sides of poncho together. A neck opening of about 14 inches will allow for an easy drape of the poncho around shoulders as well as for the poncho to be worn over the shoulder/under the opposite arm.

With RS facing, attach A and finish neckline with a round of sl st into the back vertical bar of the edge stitch. Attach A along the bottom of poncho with sl st and work a finishing row of sl st into back vertical bar of the edge stitch across bottom edge.

Cut 12"/30cm lengths of yarn to create 6"/15cm fringe. Attach fringe through vertical loops of Tss stitches at the start and end rows of the fabric.

This project was created with

4 skeins of Berroco's *Quest* in St. Barts (#9932), 100% nylon, 1.75oz/50g = approx 82yd/74m ea

4 skeins Berroco's *Optik* in Cadaquez (#4944), 48% cotton/ 21% acrylic/ 20% mohair/8% metallic/3% polyester, 1.75oz/50g = approx 87yd/78m ea

3 skeins Berroco's *Zen* in Edamame (#8123), 60% nylon/40% cotton, 1.75oz/50g = approx 110 yd/99m ea

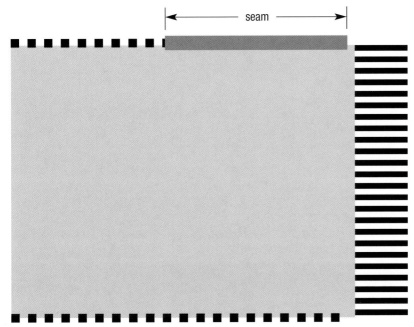

Figure 1

Paper Moon Ensemble

As delicate and fleeting as the penumbra of a lunar eclipse, this capelet and gauntlet combination worked in an exotic blend of yarn is a perfect foil for a little dressy dress.

DESIGN BY
Laurie Kimmelstiel

Capelet

Approx: 622yd/560m of linen/nylon fine novelty yarn
Approx: 40yd/36m of silk ribbon

Loosely ch 85 sts.

ROW 1: Work 1 dc into 4th ch from hk and 1 dc into ea ch across row to end. Turn.

ROW 2: Ch 4, work 1 dc into 4th ch from hk, ch 1, *then work 1 dc into same ch, ch 1. Rep from * 1 time, then ** work 1 dc in next dc, ch1, skip over one dc. Rep from ** until last dc. Then work ***1 dc, ch 1. Rep from *** one time, 1dc. Turn.

ROWS 3–6: Rep row 2, turn.

ROW 7: Ch 4, work 2 dc into 4th ch from hk . Then work 1dc into ea dc and ea ch across row to last dc. Work 3 dc into last dc. Turn.

ROW 8: Ch 4, work 1dc into 4th ch from hk , ch 1, 1dc again in same ch, then *sk one dc and work 1dc into next dc, ch 1 and rep from * across row to last dc. Work 1dc, ch 1, and 1dc into last dc. Turn.

ROW 9: Ch 4, work 1 dc into 4th ch from hk , ch 1. Then, *work 1dc into ea dc, ch 1. Rep from *across row to last dc. Work 1 dc, ch1, and 1dc into last dc. Turn.

ROW 10: Ch 4, work 1 dc into 4th ch from hk , ch 1, 1dc again in same ch, then work 1 dc in ea dc and ea ch across row to last st, work 1dc, ch 1, and 1dc into last dc. Turn.

ROW 11: Rep row 8.

ROW 12: Rep row 10.

ROW 13: Rep row 8.

ROWS 14–18: Rep row 9, but do not turn. Fasten off.

Finishing

Working with 2 strands together, carefully and loosely crochet sl st edge, working 1 sl st into ea chain across 1st row (ch row) of capelet.

Cut yarn, fasten off, and weave in ends.

Paper Moon Ensemble

Ribbon Band

ROW 1: Using silk ribbon, beg on corner on the widest edge, carefully sc along sl st edge to corner, working 2 sc at bottom corner st, continuing along bottom edge to corner, working 2 sc again in next corner st and then sc up edge to top. Turn.

ROW 2: Rep row 1. Cut ribbon, fasten off, and weave in ends securely.

With sewing needle and matching thread, sew button to top left edge of ribbon band.

Gauntlets (make 2)

Approx: 622yd/560m of linen/nylon fine novelty yarn
Approx: 40yd/36m of silk ribbon
Hooks: 3.75mm/F-5 and 6.5mm/K-10½

Pattern Note

Wind yarn in 2 separate balls. This portion of the project is worked using 2 threads at a time.

Using two strands of the paper yarn and 6.5mm/K-10½ hk, ch 4.

ROW 1: Work 2 dc into the 3rd ch from hk, 2 dc in ea of the next two ch, turn.

ROW 2: Ch 3, work 2 dc in 3rd ch from hk and 2 dc in ea dc across row to last dc, 1 dc in last dc, turn.

ROW 3: Ch 3, work 1 dc in 3rd ch from hk, 2 dc in ea dc to last dc, work 1 dc in last st. Turn.

ROW 4: Ch 3, work 1 dc in 3rd ch from hk, 1 dc in ea dc across row to last dc, 2 dc in last dc. Turn

ROW 5: Ch 3, work 1 dc in 3rd ch from hk , ch 1, * sk dc and work 1 dc into next dc, ch 1, rep from * to last st and then work 1dc, ch 1, 1 dc in last dc. Turn.

ROW 6: Ch 3, work 1 dc in 3rd ch from hk, ch 1, * sk dc and work 1 dc into next dc, ch 1, rep from * to last st and then work 1 dc in last dc. Turn.

ROW 7 (THUMBHOLE ROW): Ch 3, work 1 dc in the 3rd ch from hk, ch 1, sk one dc and work 1dc in to next dc, ch3, sk next ch, dc, ch and work 1 dc into next dc, (5th dc on row below) ch1, *sk next dc and make 1 dc over ch 1. Rep from * across row last dc, 1 dc, ch 1, 1 dc in last dc. Turn.

ROW 8: Ch 4, work 1dc in 3rd ch from hk, ch 1, 1 dc in ea dc across row until beg of thumb opening, 1 dc in ea of three ch across top of thumb opening, 1dc in next dc, ch 1, 1dc, ch 1, 1dc in last dc of row. Turn.

ROW 9: Ch 3, work 1dc in 2nd dc, ch1, *sk dc and work 1dc in next dc, ch 1. Rept from * one time. **Sk ch and work 1 dc into next dc, ch 1. Rep from ** to last dc and work 2 dc in last dc. Turn.

ROW 10: Ch 3, work 1 dc in 2nd dc, ch 1., * Sk ch, work 1dc in dc, ch1. Rep from * to 3rd dc from end of row, 1dc, skip to edge and work 1dc in last ch. Turn.

ROW 11: Ch 3, work 1 dc in 3rd dc from edge, ch 1, *sk ch work 1dc in next dc, ch 1, rep from * across row to 2nd to last dc, 1dc in next 2 dc. Turn.

ROW 12: Ch 4, sk 1 dc and 1 ch, work 1dc in next dc, ch 1. *Sk 1 ch, work 1 dc, ch 1. Rep from * across row to last dc. Work 2dc in last dc. Turn.

ROW 13: Ch 3, *sk 1 ch, work 1dc in next dc, ch 1, rep from * to last dc, 1dc. Turn.

ROW 14: Rep row 13.

ROW 15: Ch 4, work 1 dc in 1st dc, ch 1, * sk ch, 1 dc in next dc, ch 1, rep from * to last dc of row, 2 dc . Turn.

ROW 16: Ch 4, work 1dc in 1st dc, ch 1, * sk ch, 1 dc in next dc, ch 1, rep from * to last dc of row, 1 dc. Turn.

ROW 17: Ch 4, work 1dc in 1st dc, ch 1* sk ch, work 1 dc in next dc, ch 1, rep from * across row to last dc, 1 dc. Turn .

ROWS 18–21: Rep row 17.

Cut yarn, fasten off, and weave in ends.

Ruffled Cuff

Sl st ribbon, ch 3 and work 4 dc in 1st dc at forearm edge, then work 5 dc into ea ch across row. Cut and weave in ends.

Finishing

Fold each gauntlet in half for a right and left hand, according to thumb opening. Pin together, matching sts. Join using sl st (see page 000) along edge beginning 4"/10cm below top to ruffled edge. Do not sew ruffled cuff.

Fold up cuff to top of wrist, place hand inside gauntlet, then fold cuff back over arm.

Warm Whisper Shawl

What could be more comforting (or elegant) wrapped around your shoulders than this easy-to-make mohair shawl? It's the perfect project for a beginner.

DESIGN BY
Donna Hulka

■ skill level

Beginner

■ finished measurements

Approx 52 x 24"/1.3m x 61cm

Your completed shawl will be somewhat stretchy, so measurements may vary slightly.

■ you will need

Yarn A: approx 512yd/461m grey sport weight merino

Yarn B: approx 550yd/495m grey lace weight mohair

Hook: 15mm/P/Q

Tapestry needle

■ stitches used

Chain stitch (ch)

Single crochet (sc)

■ gauge

Take time to check your gauge.

6 sc = 4"/10cm

7 rows = 4"/10cm

Pattern Note

The entire shawl is worked with two strands held together: one of yarn A and one of yarn B.

Pattern

Work a foundation chain of 81 ch, turn.

ROW 1: Sc in 2nd ch from hk and in ea ch across (80 sc), turn.

ROW 2: Ch 1, sc in 1st sc and in ea sc across (80 sc), turn.

Repeat row 2 until all yarn has been used or until shawl reaches desired size. Fasten off and weave in ends.

This project was created with

Yarn A: Gem's *Merino Opal* in Cloud Grey, 100% merino wool, ½lb/225gr cone = approx 512yd/461m

Yarn B: 5 balls of Le Fibre Nobili's *Imperiale Super Kid Mohair* (#4109), 80% mohair/20% polyamide, approx 1oz/25 = approx 110yd/100m ea

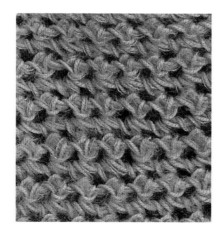

Soft As Moss Poncho

The woodsy colors of pale lichens and moss tint this delicate poncho. It's crocheted in the round from the neck down in a delightful-to-wear silk and cashmere blend yarn. Don't worry: The lacey stitch looks intricate, but it's deceptively simple to create.

DESIGN BY
Katherine Lee

Pattern

Using yarn A, ch 168, join with a sl st to 1st ch to form ring.

RND 1: Ch 3 (counts as 1 dc), 1 dc in next ch, ch 2, 1 dc in ea of next 2 ch, *(sk 2 ch, 1 dc in ea of next 3 ch, ch 3, 1 dc in next ch)13 times*, sk 2 ch, 1 dc in ea of next 2 ch, ch 2, 1 dc in ea of next 2 ch, rep from * to * once, join with a sl st to top of ch-3.

RND 2: (Inc rnd) Sl st in next dc, sl st in next ch-2 sp, ch 3 (counts as 1 dc), (1 dc, ch 2, 2 dc) in same sp, (1 dc, ch 3, 3 dc) in sp between next 2nd and 3rd dcs, [(1 dc, ch 3, 3 dc) in next ch-3 sp] 13 times, (1 dc, ch 3, 3 dc) in sp between next 1st and 2nd dc's, (2 dc, ch 2, 2 dc) in next ch-2 sp, (1dc, ch 3, 3 dc) in sp between next 2nd and 3rd dc's, [(1 dc, ch 3, 3 dc) in next ch-3 sp] 13 times, (1 dc, ch 3, 3 dc) in sp between next 1st and 2nd dc's, join with a sl st to top of ch 3.

RND 3: Sl st in next dc, sl st in next ch-2 sp, ch 3 (counts as 1 dc), (1 dc, ch 2, 2 dc) in same sp, *[(3 dc, ch 3, 1 dc) in next ch-3 sp] 15 times*, (2 dc, ch 2, 2 dc) in next ch-2 sp; rep from * to * once, join with a sl st to top of ch-3. Fasten off.

Change to yarn B.

RND 4: Sl st in next dc, sl st in next ch-2 sp, ch 3 (counts as 1 dc), (1 dc, ch 2, 2 dc) in same sp, *[(1 dc, ch 3, 3 dc) in next ch-3 sp] 15 times*, (2 dc, ch 2, 2 dc) in next ch-2 sp; rep from * to * once, join with a sl st to top of ch-3.

RND 5: (inc rnd) Sl st in next dc, sl st in next ch-2 sp, ch 3 (counts as 1 dc), (1 dc, ch 2, 2 dc) in same sp, (3 dc, ch 3, 1 dc) in sp between next 2nd and 3rd dcs, [(3 dc, ch 3, 1 dc) in next ch-3 sp] 15 times, (3 dc, ch 3, 1 dc) in sp between next 3rd and 4th dcs), (2 dc, ch 2, 2 dc) in next ch-2 sp, (3 dc, ch 3, 1 dc) in sp between next 2nd and 3rd dc's, [(3 dc, ch 3, 1 dc) in next ch-3 sp] 15 times, (3 dc, ch 3, 1 dc) in sp between next 3rd and 4th dc's, join with a sl st to top of ch-3.

RND 6: Sl st in next dc, sl st in next ch-2 sp, ch 3 (counts as 1 dc), (1 dc, ch 2, 2 dc) in same sp, *[(1 dc, ch 3, 3 dc) in next ch-3 sp] 17 times*, (2 dc, ch 2, 2 dc) in next ch-2 sp; rep from * to * once, join with a sl st to top of ch-3.

RND 7: Sl st in next dc, sl st in next ch-2 sp, ch 3 (counts as 1 dc), (1 dc, ch 2, 2 dc) in same sp, *[(3 dc, ch 3, 1 dc) in next ch-3 sp] 17 times*, (2 dc, ch 2, 2 dc) in next ch-2 sp; rep from * to * once, join with a sl st to top of ch-3. Fasten off.

Change to yarn C.

RND 8 (INC RND): Rep rnd 2, but work instructions in brackets 17 times.

■ **skill level**

Intermediate

■ **finished measurements**

Approx 14"/36cm long at center (without fringe)

Approx 30"/76cm around neck opening

■ **you will need**

Yarn A: approx 292yd/263m wool/silk blend sock, fingering, or baby weight yarn in green

Yarn B: approx 292yd/263m wool/silk blend sock, fingering, or baby weight yarn in light green

Yarn C: approx 146yd/121m wool/silk blend sock, fingering, or baby weight yarn in off-white

Hook: 5mm/H-8 or size needed to obtain gauge

Tapestry needle

■ **stitches used**

Chain stitch (ch)

Double crochet (dc)

■ **gauge**

Take time to check your gauge.

5 (1 dc, ch 3, 3 dc) groups = 5½"/14cm

2 rows = 11/4"/3cm over pattern stitch

Soft As Moss Poncho

RND 9: Rep rnd 7, but work instructions in brackets 19 times. Fasten off.

Change to yarn B.

RND 10: Rep rnd 6, but work instructions in brackets 19 times.

RND 11 (INC RND): Rep rnd 5, but work instructions in brackets 19 times. Fasten off.

Change to yarn A.

RND 12: Rep rnd 6, but work instructions in brackets 21 times.

RND 13: Rep rnd 7, but work instructions in brackets 21 times.

RND 14 (INC RND): Rep rnd 2, but work instructions in brackets 21 times.

RND 15: Rep rnd 7, but work instructions in brackets 23 times.

RND 16: Rep rnd 6, but work instructions in brackets 23 times. Fasten off.

Change to yarn C.

RND 17 (INC RND): Rep rnd 5, but work instructions in brackets 23 times.

RND 18: Rep rnd 6, but work instructions in brackets 25 times.

RND 19: Rep rnd 7, but work instructions in brackets 25 times. Fasten off.

Change to yarn B.

RND 20 (INC RND): Rep rnd 2, but work instructions in brackets 25 times. Fasten off.

Change to yarn A.

RND 21: Rep rnd 7, but work instructions in brackets 27 times.

RND 22: Rep rnd 6, but work instructions in brackets 27 times. Fasten off.

Change to yarn B.

RND 23 (INC RND): Rep rnd 5, but work instructions in brackets 27 times. Fasten Off.

Finishing

Lightly block poncho (see page 000). Weave in all ends.

Neck Edging

With yarn B, working in opposite side of foundation chain round, work 1 sc in every other ch along neck opening, join with a sl st to 1st sc. Fasten off.

Fringe

Cut 11"/28cm lengths of yarn B for fringe. Using 3 strands for ea fringe group, attach 1 group to ea ch-2 and ch-3 sp along bottom edge (see page 000). Trim as needed.

This project was created with

2 balls of *Richesse et Soie* in Moss (#9521), 65% cashmere/35% silk, .875oz/25g = approx 146yd/134m ea

2 balls of *Richesse et Soie* in Pale Moss (#9510), 65% cashmere/35% silk, .875oz/25g = approx 146yd/134m ea

1 ball of *Richesse et Soie* in Ivory (#9146), 65% cashmere/35% silk, .875oz/25g = approx146yd/134m

Fanciful Additions

Petticoat Ruffle and Blossom Charms

Add a lot of style (with very little effort!) to your favorite little denim skirt. The lacey, pale blue edge appears to be a petticoat playfully peeking out from under the skirt. Dangle the blossom charms from a carabiner on your belt loops for an up-to-date look.

DESIGN BY
Nancy Minsky

Petticoat Ruffle and Blossom Charms

Ruffle

- **skill level**

    Easy

- **finished measurements**

    Approx 4"/10cm for the ruffle

    Approx 2"/5cm for each blossom ruffle

- **you will need**

    Denim skirt

    Color A: approx 75yd/68m denim variegated medium weight cotton yarn

    Color B: approx 138yd/125m bright blue light weight cotton yarn

    Color C: 156yd/140m pale blue medium weight linen/nylon blend yarn

    Hook: 5mm/H-8

    Tapestry needle

    Sewing needle and matching thread

- **stitches used**

    Chain stitch (ch)

    Slip stitch (sl st)

    Single crochet (sc)

    Double crochet (dc)

    Triple crochet (tr)

- **special stitch pattern**

    Make group: (tr, ch 1, tr, ch 1, tr, ch 1, tr) into same st

- **gauge**

    Gauge is not crucial in this pattern.

Pattern Note

The ruffle will be worked in the round.

With yarn A, ch enough stitches to go around the hem edge of the skirt. Join with a sl st into a ring.

Ruffle

RND 1: Sc into every ch to starting sc, join with sl st in 1st sc.

NOTE: Check the fit of your crochet work on the skirt hem before continuing. If the size needs adjustment, do it now. The finished ruffle will add 4"/10cm to the length of your skirt. Try on the denim skirt and shorten hem as needed to achieve the desired finished length with ruffle.

RND 2: Ch 1, *dc into next st, cont from * around, join to beg ch 1, ch 3.

RND 3: Tr into next st, *ch 1, tr into next st, cont from *around to beg ch 3, join, cut yarn and fasten off..

RND 4: Pick up and join yarn B. Ch 1, *sc into next st, cont from* around to beg ch 1, join, ch 3.

RND 5: Sk 2 st, *make group into next st, sk 2 st, dc into next st, cont from * around to beg ch 3, join, ch 3.

RND 6: Sk 2 st, *make 5 tr into middle ch of group, dc into next dc, cont from *around to beg ch 3, join, cut yarn, and fasten off.

RND 7: Pick up and join yarn A. Ch 1, *sc into next st, cont from *around to beg ch 1, join, cut yarn, and fasten off.

RND 8: Pick up and join yarn C. Ch 2, sk 2 st, *dc 3 times into next st, sk 1 st, sc into next st, sk 1 st, cont from * around to beginning ch 2, join.

RND 9: Ch 1, *(sc into space between next 2 dc, ch 3, sc into same space) 3 times, sc into next st, sk 2 sts cont from * around to beginning ch 1, join and fasten off.

Finishing

Use tapestry needle to weave in all yarn ends.

Gently steam and block the ruffle as needed.

Pin ruffle with ⅜"/1 cm overlap to the hem edge. Hand stitch the top edge of the ruffle using a back stitch.

Charms

Pattern Note

Each charm is made up of one large center and two small centers.

Large Center

Work large center using one strand of cotton yarn and one strand of metallic yarn held together.

Using a 4mm/G-6 hk, ch 5, sl st to 1st ch to form a ring.

RND 1: Make 10 sc into ring, join with sl st to 1st sc.

RND 2: *Ch 4, 4 dtr into same sc leaving last lp of each dtr on hk, yo and pull through 5 lps, ch 4, sl st firmly into same sc, sl st into next ch, sl st into next sc, rep from * 3 more times; ch 4, 4 dtr into same sc leaving last lp of each dtr on hk, yo and pull through 5 lps firmly, ch 4, sl st firmly into same sc, sl st into next st (5 petals finished).

Stem

Ch 20, turn, sl st into 2nd ch from hk, sl st into ea following ch, join with sl st into ring, sl st into next st, ch 1, cut yarns, and fasten off. Vary the length of additional stems with ch 10 and ch 15.

Small Center (make 2)

Work small center with 1 strand cotton yarn.

Using a 3.5mm/E-4 hk, ch 5, sl st to 1st ch to form a ring.

RND 1: Make 10 sc into ring, join with sl st to 1st sc.

RND 2: *Ch 4, 4 dtr into same sc leaving last lp of each dtr on hk, yo and pull through 5 lps , ch 4, sl st firmly into same sc, sl st into next ch, sl st into next st, repeat from * 3 more times; ch 4, 4 dtr into same sc leaving last lp of each dtr on hk, yo and pull through 5 lps firmly, ch 4, sl st firmly into same sc, sl st into next st (5 petals finished), sl st into next st, cut yarn, and fasten off.

Finishing

With a tapestry needle, neatly secure all yarn ends.

Fold stem end and hand stitch to form a loop. Slip stem loop onto split ring.

Fluff petals of small centers to add dimension. Stitch small centers to large center with matching thread.

Slip charms onto key ring.

Blossom Charms

■ **skill level**

Easy

■ **you will need**

Approx 33yd/30m fine cotton yarn for each blossom in orange, yellow, or dark pink

Approx 33yd/30m fine metallic yarn for each blossom

Hooks: 3.5mm/E-4, 4mm/G-6

½"/1cm split rings

Snap bolt key ring

Tapestry needle

■ **stitches used**

Chain stitch (ch)

Slip stitch (sl st)

Single crochet (sc)

Double treble crochet (dtr)

This project was created with

Ruffle

1 ball Debbie Bliss *Cotton Denim* in Aran (#14503), 100% cotton, 1.75oz/50g = approx 75yd/68m

1 ball Schachenmayr's *Nomotta* in Blue Jeans (#52), 100% cotton, 1.75oz/50g = approx 183yd/125m

1 ball *GGH* in Safari (#29), 78% linen/22% nylon, 1.75oz/50 g = approx 156yd/140

Blossom Charms

1 ball each of Schachenmayr's *Catania* in pink (#114), orange (#189), yellow (#204), 100% cotton, 1.75oz/50g = approx 138yd/125m

1 ball each of Rowan *Lurex Shimmer* in claret (#331), copper (#330), 80% viscose/20% polyester, approx 1/oz/25g = approx 105yd/95m

Bohemian Rhapsody Ensemble

Add these romantic cuffs with an alluring and feminine design to a basic cotton tee. Pair the top with your favorite style of jeans (or skirt) strewn with blossom appliqués and you have a stylish, bohemian ensemble perfect for a stroll along the Left Bank.

DESIGN BY
Nancy Minsky

Pattern Note
This pattern is worked in the round.

Cuffs (make 2)

Using the 3.25mm/D-3 hk and yarn A, ch 39, join with sl st to 1st ch to form ring.

RND 1: Ch 1, work sc into ea ch st, join with a sl st into beg ch 1.

RND 2: Repeat rnd 1.
Tip: When you finish rnd 2 check the fit. Slip on the T-shirt and pull on the crocheted loop, so that it lies on the edge of the cuff. It should fit smoothly on the hem. If you find it too tight or too loose, now is the time to make adjustments in the size. Unravel the work and restart the project, adding or subtracting chains in the foundation row.

RND 3: Ch 3, *work tr into next sc, ch 1, sk next sc, rep from * until beg ch 3, join with sl st.

RNDS 4–10: Ch 3, *work tr into next sp, ch 1, rep from * until beg ch 3 and join with sl st. Allow yarn to hang down back side of cuff.

RND 11: Join yarn B. Ch 1, *sc into next sp, ch 1, rep from * until beg ch 1 and join. Cut yarn leaving a 6"/15cm tail and fasten off.

RND 12: Pick up yarn A and join, ch 2, *dc into next ch 1 sp, ch 1, dc into same sp, ch 1, dc into same sp, sc into next ch 1 sp, rep from * until beg ch 2 and join. Allow yarn to hang down back side of cuff.

RND 13: Join yarn C. Ch 1, *sk next lp and sc under next lp, ch 3, sk next ch 1 sp, sc into next ch 1 sp, rep from* until beg ch 1 and join. Cut yarn, leaving a 6"/15cm tail and fasten off.

RND 14: Pick up and join yarn A. Ch 3, *work a group (tr, ch 1, tr, ch 1, tr) into sp of ea ch 3 loops, rep from * until beg ch 3, join.

Bohemian Rhapsody Ensemble

RNDS 15–16: Ch 3, *work a group (tr, ch 1, tr, ch 1, tr) into sp between 2 groups, rep from* until beg ch 3, tr, ch 1, tr, ch 1, join. Cut yarn leaving a 6"/15cm tail and fasten off.

RND 17: Join yarn B. Ch 1, sc into ea sp until beg ch 1 and join. Cut yarn, leaving a 6"/15cm tail and fasten off.

RND 18: Pick up and join yarn A. *Ch 5, sc into next sp, rep from * until beg ch 5, join. Cut yarn, leaving a 6"/15cm tail and fasten off.

RND 19: Pick up and join yarn C. *Ch 3, sc under next ch 5 lp, rep from * until beg ch3, make join. Cut yarn and fasten off.

Finishing

Use a tapestry needle to neatly secure all yarn ends.

Gently steam and block the work (see page 000).

Pin crocheted cuff to the sleeve. Match join of crochet work with underarm seam. Overlap the hem of sleeve with the cuff approx ½"/1cm. Hand stitch using back stitch and matching thread along the top edge of crochet and around the bottom edge of the hem. Allow some ease in your stitching as the fabric has some stretch.

Care Note

You can machine wash this garment, but to prolong the beauty of the hand crochet it is advisable to hand wash and dry flat.

Floral Appliqués (make as many as desired)

With yarn A using 3.25mm/D-3 hk, ch 6, sl st to 1st ch to form a ring.

RND 1: Ch 3, 1 dc into center of ring. *Ch 2, (yo, insert hook into center of ring, yo and draw through, yo and draw through 2 lps on hook) twice, yo and draw through last 3 lps on hook, rep from * 6 times and end ch 2, join with sl st to 3rd ch of starting ch 3, turn.

RND 2: Ch 3, 2 dc into 1st ch-2 sp, *ch 2, 3 dc into next ch-2 sp, rep from * 6 times and end ch 2, join with sl st to 3rd ch of starting ch 3. Cut yarn and fasten off.

RND 3: With yarn C, using 5mm/H-8 hk, ch 3, 1 tr into ch-2 sp, ch 1, 1 dc into same ch-2 sp, ch 1, * make group, ch 1, rep from * 6 times, join with 1st ch of starting ch 3. Cut yarn and fasten off.

RND 4: With yarn B, using 7mm/approx K-10½ h k. Sc into every ch-1 sp, join with 1st sc. Cut yarn and fasten off.

Finishing

Use a tapestry needle to secure all yarn ends to avoid unraveling.

Gently steam and block.

Pin the appliqués, placing them where they will look the most attractive, balanced, and sophisticated. Try on the garment, with the appliqués pinned on and look at the side, back, and front views to check and adjust placement as needed.

Once you are satisfied with the placement, stitch the appliqués with thread matching the color of denim, along the outer edges and center of each blossom.

Care Note

You can machine wash this garment, but to prolong the beauty of the hand crochet it is advisable to hand wash and dry flat.

This project was created with

Yarn A: 1 skein Schachenmayr's *Nomotta* in Catania (#105), 100% cotton, 1.75oz/50g = approx 138yd/125m

Yarn B: 1 ball Rowan's *All Season's Cotton* (#163), 60 % cotton/40% acrylic, 1oz/25 grams = approx 50yd/45 m

Yarn C: 1 skein Rowan's *Cotton Braid* (351), 68% cotton/22% viscose/10% linen, 1oz/25g = approx 28yd/25m

Diamond Mesh Overskirt

Slipping this mesh overskirt over a simple unadorned skirt is a great magic trick. Abracadabra!

DESIGN BY
Donna Hulka

■ **skill level**

Experienced

■ **finished measurements**

Small: waist 25½"/65cm, hip 34"/86cm

Medium: waist 28½"/72cm, hip 38"/97cm

Large: waist 31½"/80cm, hip 42"/107cm

Extra Large: waist 34½"/88cm, hip 46"/117cm

■ **you will need**

418yd (418, 523, 523)/380m (380(418yd/380m, 523yd/475m, 523yd/475m) worsted or heavy worsted weight silk yarn

Hook: 5mm/H-8 or size needed to obtain gauge

Stitch markers (optional)

Approx 1½"/4cm wide sport elastic to fit waist comfortably

Straight pins

Tapestry needle

Sewing needle and matching thread

■ **stitches used**

Chain stitch (ch)

Single crochet (sc)

■ **gauge**

Take time to check your gauge.

16 st and 16 rows in waistband = 4"/10cm

Pattern Notes

It's helpful to use stitch markers to mark the first and last stitch of each round. This will help you keep your place while working the waistband. When working into a chain, be sure to insert your hook under the top two strands.

Waistband

Ch 102 (114, 126, 138), sl st in 1st ch to form a ring.

RND 1(RS): Ch 1. Sc in same ch as sl st, (ch 1, sk next ch, sc in next ch) around to last ch, sc in last ch, sl st in 1st sc to join [102 (114, 126, 138) sc and ch-1 sp].

RND 2: Ch 1, sc in same sc as sl st, (sc in next ch-1 sp, ch 1) around to last 2 sc, sk next sc, sc in last sc, sl st in 1st sc to join [102 (114, 126, 138) sc and ch-1 sp].

RND 3: Ch 1, sc in same sc as sl st, (ch 1, sc in next ch-1 sp) around to last st, sc in last sc, sl st in 1st sc to join [102 (114, 126, 138) sc and ch-1 sp].

RNDS 4–7: Rep rnds 2–3 twice.

ROUND 8: Rep rnd 2.

Skirt

RND 9: Ch 1. Sc in same sc as sl st, sc in next sc, [*ch 5, sk next (ch-1 sp, sc, and ch-1 sp)*, sc in each of next (sc, ch-1 sp, and sc)] around ending with: rep from * to * once, sc in last sc, sl st in 1st sc to join [17 (19, 21, 23) ch-5 sp].

RND 10: Ch 1, sc in same sc as sl st, [*ch 3, sk next (sc and 2 ch), sc in 3rd ch of ch 5, ch 3*, sk next (2 ch and sc), sc in next sc] around, ending with: rep from * to * once, sl st in 1st ch to join [34 (38, 42, 46) ch-3 sp].

RND 11: Ch 6, sk next 2 ch, [*sc in each of (3rd ch of ch 3, next sc, and 1st ch of ch 3)*, ch 5, sk next (2 ch, sc, and 2 ch)] around, ending with: rep from * to * once, ch 2, sl st in 4th ch of beg ch 6 to join [16 (18, 20, 22) ch-5 sp plus 2 ch-2 sp at end of rnd].

Diamond Mesh Overskirt

RND 12: Ch 1, sc in same ch as sl st, [*ch 3, sk next (2 ch and sc), sc in next sc, ch 3*, sk next (sc and 2 ch), sc in 3rd ch of ch 5] around, ending with: rep from * to * once, sl st in 1st sc to join [34 (38, 42, 46) ch-3 sp].

RND 13: Ch 1, sc in same sc as sl st, sc in 1stt ch of ch 3, [*ch 5, sk next (2 ch, sc, and 2 ch)*, sc in each of (3rd ch of ch 3, next sc, and 1st ch of ch 3)] around, ending with: rep from * to * once, sc in last ch, sl st in 1st sc to join [17 (19, 21, 23) ch-5 sp].

RND 14: Rep rnd 10.

RND 15: Ch 8, sk next 2 ch, [*sc in each of (3rd ch of ch 3, next sc, and 1st ch of ch 3)*, ch 7, sk next (2 ch, sc, and 2 ch)] around, ending with: rep from * to * once, ch 3, sl st in 5th ch of beg ch 8 to join [16 (18, 20, 22) ch-7 plus 2 ch-3 sp].

RND 16: Ch 1, sc in same ch as sl st, [*ch 4, sk next (3 ch and sc), sc in next sc, ch 4*, sk next (sc and 3 ch), sc in 4th ch of ch 7] around, ending with: rep from * to * once, sl st in 1st sc to join [34 (38, 42, 46) ch-4 sp].

RND 17: Ch 1, sc in same ch as sl st, sc in 1st ch of ch 4, [*ch 7, sk next (3 ch, sc, and 3 ch)*, sc in each of (4th ch of ch 4, next sc, and 1st ch of ch 4)] around, ending with: rep from * to * once, sc in last ch, sl st in 1st sc to join [17 (19, 21, 23) ch-7 sp].

RND 18: Ch 1, sc in same sc as sl st, [*ch 4, sk next (sc and 3 ch), sc in 4th ch of ch 7, ch 4*, sk next (3 ch and sc), sc in next sc] around, ending with: rep from * to * once, sl st in 1st sc to join [34 (38, 42, 46) ch-4 sp].

RND 19: Ch 8, sk next 3 ch, [*sc in each of (4th ch of ch 4, next sc, and 1st ch of ch 4)*, ch 7, sk next (3 ch, sc, and 3 ch)] around, ending with: rep from * to * once, ch 3, sl st in 5th ch of beg ch 8, to join [16 (18, 20, 22) ch-7 sps plus 2 ch-3 sps].

RNDS 20–23: Rep rnds 16–19.

RND 24: Rep rnd 16.

RND 25: Ch 1, sc in same sc as sl st, sc in 1st ch of ch 4, [*ch 9, sk next (3 ch, sc, and 3 ch)*, sc in each of (4th ch of ch 4, next sc, and 1st ch of ch 4)] around, ending with: rep from * to * once, sc in last ch, sl st in 1st sc to join [17 (19, 21, 23) ch-9 sps].

RND 26: Ch 1, sc in same sc as sl st, [*ch 5, sk next (sc and 4 ch), sc in 5th ch of ch 9, ch 5*, sk next (4 ch and sc), sc in next sc] around, ending with: rep from * to * once, sl st in 1st sc to join [34 (38, 42, 46) ch-5 sp].

RND 27: Ch 10, sk next 4 ch, [*sc in each of (5th ch of ch 5, next sc, and 1st ch of ch 5)*, ch 9, sk next (4 ch, sc, and 4 ch)] around, ending with: rep from * to * once, ch 4, sl st in 6th ch of beg ch 10 to join [16 (18, 20, 22) ch-9 sp plus 2 ch-4 sp].

RND 28: Ch 1, sc in same ch as sl st, [*ch 5, sk next (4 ch and sc), sc in next sc, ch 5*, sk next (sc and 4 ch), sc in 5th ch of ch 9] around, ending with: rep from * to * once, sl st in 1st sc to join [34 (38, 42, 46) ch-5 sps].

RND 29: Ch 1, sc in same sc as sl st, sc in 1st ch of ch 4, [*ch 9, sk next (4 ch, sc, and 4 ch)*, sc in each of (5th ch of ch 5, next sc, and 1st ch of ch 5)] around, ending with: rep from * to * once, sc in last ch, sl st in 1st sc to join [17 (19, 21, 23) ch-9 sps].

RNDS 30–45: Rep rnds 26–29 four times.

RND 46: Rep rnd 26.

RND 47: Ch 6, sk next 4 ch, [*sc in each of (5th ch of ch 5, next sc, and 1st ch of ch 5)*, ch 6, sk next (4 ch, sc, and 4 ch)] around, ending with: rep from * to * once, ch 3, sl st in 3rd ch of beg ch 6 to join. Fasten off and weave in ends.

This project was created with

4 (4, 5, 5) balls of Plymouth's *Turino Silk* (#01), 100% silk, 1.75oz/50g = approx 103yd/95m ea

Finishing

Cut elastic to waist measurement, plus ½"/1cm seam allowance. Hand stitch elastic into a circle. Mark elastic into 4 equal sections.

Mark wrong side of the skirt waistband into 4 equal sections.

Pin the elastic inside the waistband, matching marked points. Place the skirt on a flat surface. Ease the crocheted waistband until the waistband and elastic are even with each other. Once they are even, it may help to pin the center of the section, dividing it in two. With sewing thread and needle, whipstitch top and bottom of elastic to waistband. Repeat for each section until elastic is completely sewn in.

Impanema Ensemble

Can you hum or whistle the melody?
Do you remember the lyrics?

This ensemble is guaranteed to turn heads as you pass by on the shore, the pool, or at the spa. If a bikini isn't your style, the wrap makes a perfect shawl to wear with anything your heart desires.

DESIGN BY
Kalpna Kapoor

■ **skill level**

Bikini: Intermediate

Wrap: Beginner

■ **finished measurements**

Top: To fit bra cup sizes A (B, C)

Bottom: One size fits most

Wrap: One size fits most

■ **you will need** (bikini)

Yarn A: Approx 528yd (528, 704)/480m (480, 640) of stretchy cotton/polyester chunky weight yarn in blue

Yarn B: Approx 61yd (61,122)/55m (55,109) of cotton/nylon/acrylic sport weight yarn in a variegated color

Hook: 3.5mm/E-4 or size needed to obtain gauge

Approx 1/2yd/.5m fabric (optional lining)

Elastic thread for bikini bottom

Sewing needle

Tapestry needle

■ **stitches used**

Chain stitch (ch)

Single crochet (sc)

Half double crochet (hdc)

■ **gauge**

Take time to check your gauge.

20 hdc and 25 rows = 4"/10cm

Bikini Bra Cups (make 2)

With yarn A, ch 15 (16, 20).

ROW 1(RS) : 1 hdc in 2nd ch from hook. 1 hdc in each ch to last ch. Mark center hdc. Do not turn. Working into other side of ch, work 1 hdc in each rem loop of ch to end of ch. Turn. [31 (33–41) hdc].

ROW 2: Ch 2. 1 hdc in each hdc to end of row. Turn.

ROW 3: Ch 2. 1 hdc in each hdc to center hdc. 5 (5,3) hdc in center hdc. 1 hdc in each hdc to end of row. Turn.

ROW 4: Rep row 2.

ROW 5: Ch 2. 1 hdc in each hdc to center hdc. 3 hdc in center hdc. 1 hdc in each hdc to end of row. Turn.

Rep last 4 rows 4(5,6) times more, then 2nd row once more. 61 (69, 69) hdc.

Joining Cups

With WS of work facing, work 28 (28, 30) sc evenly across bottom of first cup. Ch 4. Work 28 (28, 30) sc evenly across bottom of second cup. Turn.

NEXT ROW (RS): Ch 1,1 sc in each of next 28(28, 30) sc. 1 sc in each of next 4 ch. 1 sc in each of next 28(28, 30) sc. Fasten off.

Bikini Bottom

With yarn A, ch 55.

ROW 1: 1 hdc in 2nd ch from hk. 1 hdc in ea ch to end of ch. (54 hdc) Turn.

ROW 2: Ch 2. 1 hdc in ea hdc to end of row. Turn.

Rep last row 7 times more.

Impanema Ensemble

Back shaping

ROW 1: Ch 20 (Yo ,draw up a loop in next st) twice, yo and draw through all loops on hook (hdc2tog made). 1 hdc in each hdc to last 2 hdc. Hdc2tog over last 2 hdc. Turn.

ROW 2: Ch 2. 1 hdc in first st, 1 hdc in each st to end of row. Turn.

Rep last 2 rows until there are 14 hdc, ending with RS facing for next row.

NEXT ROW: Ch 2. 1 hdc in each hdc to end of row. Turn.

Rep last row 15 times more.

Front shaping

NEXT ROW: Ch 2. 2 hdc in first st. 1 hdc in each st to last st. 2 hdc in last st. Turn.

NEXT 2 ROWS: Ch 2. 1 hdc in each st to end of row. Turn

Rep last 3 rows 12 times more. Fasten off.

This project was created with

3(3,4) balls of Lana Grosso's *Elastico* in #9, 96%cotton/4% polyester, 1.75oz/50g balls = approx 176yd/160m ea

4 balls of Classic Elite's *Bubbles* in Mountain Dew (#2435), cotton/nylon/acrylic, 1.75oz/50g = approx 61yd/55m each

Back Edging

With RS of work facing, sl st in first ch of foundation ch on back. Ch 1, sc in each st of foundation ch. Turn

NEXT ROW: Ch 1, sc in each st across back. Fasten off.

Rep for front edging.

Leg Edging

ROW 1: With RS of work facing, join yarn with sl st to front side edge, ch 1. Work 1 row sc evenly along leg opening. Turn.

ROW 2: Ch 1, sc in each sc to end of row. Fasten off.

Rep for second leg edging, joining yarn with sl st to back side edge.

Finishing

Thread elastic thread through first sc row of back, front, and leg edgings.

Twisted cords
(make 4 for top and 4 for bikini bottom)

1. Cut 8 strands each of color A and B each 60"/152cm long. Holding one of each strand together, with one person on either end, twist strands to the right until they begin to curl. Fold the 2 ends together and tie in a knot so they will not unravel. The strand will now twist together to make a cord. Repeat for each pair of strands.

2. Thread 2 cords through outside corners of the cups to make ties and 1 each on top corner of each cup to make the neck tie.

3. Thread 4 twisted cords to each side of front and back edging.

Optional Lining

You may prefer to line the bikini bottom. If so, cut the lining material following the middle part of the bottom, place it on the reverse side of the front crocheted section, fitting the edges,, and sew on, folding under the fabric edges by 1/2"/1cm.

Wrap

Beg at bottom point, ch 5.

ROW 1: Dc in 5th ch from hook (counts as V-st); turn.

ROW 2: Ch 4 (counts as dc and 1 ch), dc in first dc, V-st in 3rd ch of tch; turn.

ROW 3: Ch 4 (counts as dc and 1 ch), dc in first dc, V-st in sp between 2 V-sts, V-st in 3rd ch of tch; turn.

ROW 4: Ch 4 (counts as dc and 1 ch), dc in first dc, (V-st in sp between 2 V-sts) 2 times, V-st in 3rd ch of tch; turn.

ROW 5: Ch 4 (counts as dc and 1 ch); dc in first dc, (V-st in sp between 2 V-sts) 3 times, V-st in 3rd ch of tch; turn.

Cont in this pattern, working 1 more V-st between V-sts every row until there are 36 total V-sts in last row. Fasten off.

Finishing

With RS facing, join yarn with sl st in any corner, ch 1, *sc in next st; rep from * around, working 3 sc in each corner; join with a sl st to first sc. Fasten off.

■ **finished measurements**

Approx 28 x 67"/71cm x 1.7m

■ **you will need**   (wrap)

Approx 244yd/220m worsted weight yarn

Hook: 8mm/L-11 or size needed to obtain gauge

Tapestry needle

■ **stitches used**

Chain stitch (ch)

Double crochet (dc)

Slip stitch (sl st)

V-stitch (V-st)

■ **gauge**

Take time to check your gauge.

3 V-st and 5 rows = 4"/10cm

■ **special pattern stitch**

V-st: In same st work dc, ch 1, dc.

Liquid Copper Sarong

The metallic yarn of this sarong clings to the body like liquid copper and swings ever-so-seductively as you walk. This project is an excellent introduction to making a mesh pattern.

DESIGN BY
Nancy Minsky

■ **skill level**

Intermediate

■ **finished measurements**

Approx 31 x 31"/79 x 79cm (not including the ties)

■ **you will need**

Yarn A: 624yd/562m metallic yarn in copper

Yarn B: 104yd/94m metallic yarn in bronze/gold

Crochet hooks: 3.25mm/D-3,4mm/G-6, 9mm/M/N-13 or sizes needed to obtain gauge

Tapestry needle

■ **stitches used**

Chain stitch (ch)

Single crochet (sc)

Double crochet (dc)

Triple crochet (tr)

■ **gauge**

Take time to check your gauge.

Using 3.25mm/D-3: approx 10 st = 3"/8cm

Pattern Notes

Metallic yarns have a tendency to come unrolled as you work. Try unwinding several yards/meters at a time, then slip a rubber band around the ball while you crochet.

Join new balls at the row edges, in a ch-1 stitch.

Hip Band

Using yarn A and 3.25mm/D-3 hk, ch 154 (approx 46"/1.2m).

RND 1: Ch 1, work sc into each ch st all around both sides of the ch, join with a sl st into beginning ch 1, ch 2 (counts as tch).

RND 2: Work dc into ea sc, working 2 sc into each st at the four corners of the hip band, join with sl st, ch 2.

RNDS 3–4: Rep rnd 2.

RND 5: Work dc into next 25 st (or for 7"/18cm), ch 3, tr into next st, *ch 1, sk 1 st, tr into next st*, rep between * * 49 times (or for approx 26"/66 cm). Turn. You will continue to work back and forth, and no longer in the round, for the rest of the skirt.

Skirt

ROW 6: Change to 9mm/M/N-13 hk.

Ch 3, tr into next ch-1 sp, *ch 1, tr into next ch-1 sp* rep between * * until end of row. Turn.

Work 24 rows as above or until skirt measures approx 28"/71cm from bottom of hip band. Cut yarn and fasten off.

Ruffled Hem and Side Edges

Crochet around the edge of the skirt, from point where the skirt joins the hip band to the opposite point.

RND 1: Change to 3.25mm/D-3 hk. Use yarn A.

Liquid Copper Sarong

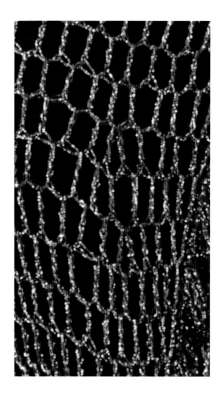

Sl st into lp on hip band and then work along side edges of sskirt, *(ch 1, sc into sp) 3 times into same sp* repeat between * * around, (ch 1, sc) 5 times into corner spaces at skirt bottom. Join with sl st into lp on hip band. Turn.

RND 2: Change to 9mm/M/N-13 hk.
Sl st into next lp on hip band. Working around the skirt edge, ch 3, tr into next ch-1 sp, *ch 1, tr into next ch-1 sp* repeat between * * until reaching hip band. Ch 3, join with sl st into 2nd loop on hip band. Turn work.

RND 3: Change to yarn B.
Sl st into next loop on hip band. Working around the skirt edge, *ch 2, dc into next ch-1 sp, * ch 1, dc into next ch-1 sp*, rep between * * until reaching hip band. Ch 2, join with sl st into next lp on hip band, cut yarn, and fasten off. Turn.

RND 4: Change to yarn A.
Sl st into same loop as rnd 3 on hip band. Working around the skirt edge, ch 3, tr into next ch-1 sp, *(ch 1, tr into next ch-1 sp), twice into same sp* repeat between * *until hip band. Ch 3, join with sl st into same loop from rnd 3 on hip band. Turn work.

RND 5 (Change to 3.25mm/D-3 hk.): Sl st into same lp as rnd 4 hip band, *(ch 1, sc into sp) twice into same sp*, rep between * * around until reach hip band, join with sl st into same lp as rnd 4 on hip band, cut yarn, and fasten off.

Belt cord (make 2):

Work with 4mm/G-6 hk, using 2 strands: 1 yarn A and 1 yarn B. Ch 2, sc in 2nd ch from hk, * insert hk under single top strand at left edge of last sc made, yo and draw through a lp (2 lps on hk), yo and through the 2 lps on hk*, repeat from * until cord measures 60"/152cm. Cut yarns and fasten off.

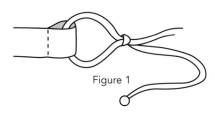

Figure 1

Finishing

Weave in all yarn ends.

Gently steam, being careful to maintain the ruffled edges.

Fold back hip band 1"/2.5cm on one end and sew using a tapestry needle and yarn A to form a loop. Slide 1 cord halfway through a loop (figure 1). Repeat on opposite side of hip band. Knot cords to secure in loops.

This project was created with

Yarn A: 6 balls of Rowan's *Lurex Shimmer* in copper (#330), 80% viscose/20% polyester, approx 3/4oz/25g = approx 104yd/94m ea

Yarn B: 1 ball of Rowan's *Lurex Shimmer* in bronze (#335), 80% viscose/20% polyester, approx 3/4oz/25g = approx 104yd/94m

Jammin' Jeans

DESIGN BY
Donna Hulka

Grab your board (whether it's surf or skate) and jam on in these jeans. Or hop in the van, pick up the kids, and complete your after school errands. Either way, you're stylin'.

Jammin' Jeans

■ **skill level**

Intermediate

■ **finished measurements**

Approx 5"/13cm

■ **you will need**

1 pair of Capri jeans*

Yarn A: approx 100yd/90m variegated blue worsted weight machine washable yarn

Yarn B: approx 60yd/54m beige worsted weight machine washable yarn

Hk: 5.5mm/I-9 or size needed to obtain gauge

Stitch marker

Tape measure or ruler

Awl or sharp-pointed scissors

Sharp-pointed needle with eye large enough to thread your yarn

Any style jeans may be used. Simply cut and hem to Capri length.

■ **stitches used**

Chain stitch (ch)

Slip stitch (sl st)

Single crochet (sc)

Double crochet (dc)

■ **gauge**

Take time to check your gauge.

13 sc and 16 rows = 4"/10cm

Preparation

Mark around hem at ½"/1cm intervals, approximately 1/8"/3mm above hem edge. Use an awl or sharp-pointed scissors to pierce the fabric at the marked intervals.

Thread needle with Yarn A and whipstitch loosely around hem edge, inserting needle into each hole previously made. Tie off, leaving ends to work in later.

Pattern Note

You will not turn your work except at the ends of rounds 3 and 4.

Edging

RND 1: With yarn B, sl st into any whipstitch, ch 1, 2 sc in same whipstitch, 2 sc in next whipstitch, (1 sc in next whipstitch, 2 sc in next whipstitch) 3 times, **(2 sc in next whipstitch) twice, (1 sc in next whipstitch, 2 sc in next whipstitch) 3 times**, rep from ** to ** around entire hem. (Note: It's fine if you reach the end of the hem without fully completing the final rep.)

Count the number of sc in this rnd and make a note of it; then sl st in 1st sc to join. Do not turn.

RND 2: If your number of stitches on rnd 1 is a multiple of 5, you do not need to inc on this round; otherwise, calculate the next highest multiple of 5 and inc to that number of sts on this round.

Ch1, sc in same sc as sl st and in each sc around, spacing incs (2 sc in 1 sc) evenly around (if needed, as indicated above), sl st in 1st sc to join. Do not turn.

RND 3: Ch 1, sc in same sc as sl st and in ea sc around, spacing 10 incs (2 sc in 1 sc) evenly around, sl st in 1st sc to join. Fasten off. Turn.

RND 4: Attach yarn A with a sl st in last sl st of rnd 3, sl st in next 4 sc; 1st flower: ch 7, sl st in back ridge only of 5th ch from hk (this is the flower center) (1st half of 1st petal made and 2nd petal made), *ch 4, sl st in flower center* (3rd petal made), rep from * to * once (4th petal made), ch 2, sl st in same sc in which you began this flower (2nd half of 1st petal made) (first flower made.)

sl st in next 5 sc. Next flower: ch 5, sc in center of 4th petal of previous flower (inserting hk from front to back of petal), ch 2, sl st in back loop only of 3rd ch of the ch 5 with which you began this flower (this is the flower center) (1stt half of 1st petal made and 2nd petal made), *ch 4, sl st in flower center* (3rd petal made), rep from * to * once (4th petal made), ch 2, sl st in same sc in which you began this flower (2nd half of 1st petal made) (flower made), rep from ** to ** around until you have completed the 3rd petal of the last flower;

4th petal of last flower: ch 2, sc in center of 2nd petal of 1st flower (inserting hk from back to front of petal), ch 2, sl st in flower center (4th petal made), ch 2, sl st in same sc in which you began this flower (2nd half of 1stt petal made), sl in 1st sl st to join. Fasten off. Turn.

RND 5: Attach yarn B with a sl st in center of 3rd petal of any flower, ch 4 loosely, *sl st in 3rd petal of next flower, ch 4 loosely*, rep from * to * around, sl st in 1st sl st to join. Do not turn.

RND 6: Ch 1, sc in same sl st, sc in each of next 4 ch (inserting hk through both the front and back lps of ch), *sc in next sl st, sc in each of next 4 ch*, rep from * to * around, sl st in 1st sc to join. Do not turn.

RND 7: The number of stitches you worked on rnd 6 should be equal to the number worked on rnd 3: If this number is odd, work 5 incs on this rnd; if it is even, work 6 incs on this rnd.

Ch 1, sc in same sc as sl st and in each sc around, working incs (2 sc in 1 sc) evenly around (as indicated above), in last sc switch to yarn A, sl st in 1st sc to join. Do not turn.

RND 8: Ch 4, sk sc with sl st, *sk next sc, dc in next sc, ch 1*, rep from * to * around, sl st in 3rd ch of beg ch 4 to join. Do not turn.

RND 9: Sl st in 1st ch-1 sp, ch 4, *dc in next ch-1 sp, ch-1*, rep from * to * around, sl st in 3rd ch of beg ch 4 to join. Do not turn.

RND 10: Ch 1, sc in 1st ch-1 sp, place st marker in sc just made (to help you keep your place), ch 1, *sc in next ch-1 sp, ch 1*, rep from * to * around, remove st marker, sl st in 1st sc (where st marker was) to join. Do not turn.

RNDS 11–15: Rep rnd 10 five times. At the end of rnd 15, place st marker in the ending sl st. Do not turn.

RND 16: Sl st in next ch-1 sp, *sl st in next sc, sl st in next ch-1 sp*, rep from * to * around, remove st marker, sl st in 1st sl st (where st marker was) to join. Fasten off and work in ends.

Rep pattern for second leg of jeans.

This project was created with

Yarn A: 1 skein of Plymouth's *Encore Colorspun* (#7991), 75% acrylic/25% wool, 1.75oz/50g = approx 150yd/135m

Yarn B: 1 skein Plymouth's *Encore* (#1415), 75% acrylic/25% wool, 1oz/30g = approx 60yd/54m

Topping It Off

Fanciful Mesh Sweater
You'll have no trouble making a catch when you wear this stunning, asymmetrically–styled mesh sweater.

DESIGN BY
Marty Miller

Pattern Notes

When you are working with yarn in this particular pattern stitch you may find that the material stretches. When you measure your gauge, place the fabric on a flat surface, without pulling the edges out. Your gauge will be approximate; because of the nature of the material, it won't be exact. If your gauge is off by a lot, change your hook size.

The completed garment will drape well and stretch a bit. It is meant to be somewhat loose.

The sweater is worked in one piece, from the bottom up, in rows, starting at the point. Once the bottom triangle is worked, the rows become rounds when you join the side. The body is worked up to the armholes, then the sweater is divided into front and back.

The sleeves are added on after the shoulder seams are joined. The back of the sweater is the same as the front—and there is no right or wrong side of the fabric until you get to the neck edge. Then the right side of the sweater is the last row of the neck edge.

Be sure to join the shoulder seams with the right sides of the front and back facing each other, so the seam will be on the inside.

If you want to make a larger sweater, simply crochet more rows at the beginning, until the width of the triangle is approximately the chest measurement you want. Crochet the sides in rounds up to the underarm. You may have to add more rounds. Then crochet the front and the back, adding more rows if desired.

Finally, follow the sleeve directions, again, adding more rows at the top if needed. You might want to decrease every 3rd or 4th row, or add rows to the bottom of the sleeve.

Bottom Triangle

Ch 5: (Counts as an elongated dc, ch 1 here and throughout)

ROW 1: Dc in 5th ch from hk ; (2 dc). Ch 5, turn.

ROW 2: Dc in first dc (beg inc made), ch 1, dc in next dc, ch 1, dc in 4th ch of tch, ch 1, dc in same ch of tch (end inc made); (4 dc). Ch 5, turn.

- **finished measurements**

  This sweater is designed to fit bust sizes S (34"/86cm), M (38"/96cm), and L (42"/107cm)

- **you will need**

  726yd (968, 1089)/653m (871, 980) worsted weight cotton blend yarn in yellow-green

  Hook: 6.5mm/K/10½ or size needed to obtain gauge

- **stitches used**

  Chain stitch (ch)

  Single crochet (sc)

  Double crochet (dc)

  Slip stitch (sl st)

- **special stitches**

  Picot: Ch 3, sl st in 3rd ch from hk, sk 1 sc, sl st in next sc = 1 picot

  Dec dc: Start a dc, yo, insert hk, yo, pull through, yo, pull through 2 lps on hk. Yo, insert hk in next st, yo, pull through, yo, pull through 2 loops on hk, yo, pull through all lps on hk = 1 dec dc (see page 000)

- **gauge**

  Take time to check your gauge.

  Mesh pattern: 6 pattern repeats = 6 rows = approx 4"/10cm

Fanciful Mesh Sweater

ROW 3: Dc in first dc (beg inc), ch 1, *dc in next dc, ch 1. Rep from * across to tch, dc in 4th ch of tch, ch 1, dc in same ch of tch (end inc); (6 dc). Ch 5, turn.

ROWS 4–25 (27, 31): Rep row 3; [50 (54, 62) dc]. Ch 1, join with a sl st to 4th ch of first ch 5 in the row. You will now be working in rounds. Ch 4, turn. (Ch 4 counts as dc, ch 1 here and throughout.)

RND 1: Sk the first dc, dc in the next dc, ch 1, *dc in next dc, ch 1. Rep from * around; [50 (54, 62) dc]. Join with a sl st in 3rd ch of tch. Ch 4, turn.

RNDS 2–11(13, 15): Rep rnd 1, until side measures approx. 8"(8 1/2, 10)/20cm (21, 25); join as above. Ch 4, turn.

Front

You will now be working in rows.

ROW 1: Sk the first dc, dc in the next dc, *ch 1, dc in next dc. Rep from * 22(24, 28) times; [24 (26, 30) dc]. Ch 4, turn. (Remember, the ch 4 at the beginning of each row counts as the first dc, ch 1.)

ROWS 2–11(15, 15): Rep row 1. [Row 11(15, 15) is the RS of the sweater.] Fasten off, leaving a long tail to sl st the shoulders together.

Back

Join the yarn in the last rnd before you started crocheting the front in the next dc after the last stitch of the first row of the front. Ch 4.

ROWS 1–11(15, 15): Rep the directions for the front.

Joining The Shoulders

With RS of the sweater facing each other, sl st the shoulder seams tog, going into the top lp only on each stitch. Leave about 10" (10½, 10¾)/25cm (27, 27) open in the middle for the neckline.

Edging

RND 1: From the RS, join yarn, ch 1, sc evenly along the neck edge. Join to the 1st ch with a sl st. Ch 1, do not turn.

RND 2: Sl st in same st as joining, *ch 3, sl st in 3rd ch from hk , skip 1 sc on neck edge, sl st in next sc. (1 picot made). Rep from * around. Join with sl st to 1st sl st.

Sleeves

The sleeves are worked in rounds.

RND 1: From the RS of the sweater, join the yarn in the dc on the left side of 1 of the

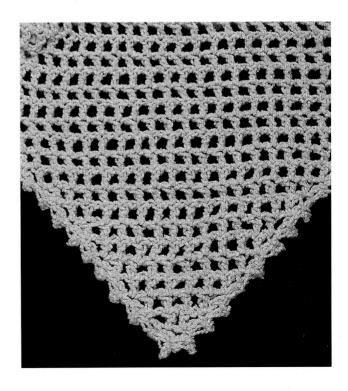

underarms. Working along the edges of the rows of the bodice, ch 4, dc in the ch st at the end of the 1st row, *ch 1, dc at the end of the next row. Rep from * around; [23 (31, 31) dc]. Join with a sl st to the third ch. Ch 4, turn.

RND 2: Sk the 1st dc, *dc in next dc, ch 1. Rep from * around. Ch 4, turn.

RNDS 3 AND 4: Rep rnd 2.

RND 5: Sk the first dc, *dc in next dc, ch 1. Rep from * around until you get to the last two dc. Dec dc in the last two dc, ch 1, join with sl st to third ch of tch; [22 (30, 30) dc]. Join as above.

RNDS 6–8: Rep rnd 2.

RND 9: Rep rnd 5; [21 (29,29) dc].

RNDS10–12: Rep rnd 2.

RND 13: Rep rnd 5; [20 (28, 28) dc].

RND 14: Rep rnd 2.

RND 15: Rep rnd 5: [19 (27, 27) dc].

RND 16: Rep rnd 2.

Continue in this manner, dec on the next rnd and in every other rnd after that until you have 23 rnds; [15 (23, 23) dc]. Fasten off. (If you want your sleeves longer, just rep rnd 2 as needed.)

Repeat these directions on the other side of the sweater for the other sleeve.

Cuff Point on Sleeve

Fold sleeve in half to find the middle dc that lines up with the shoulder seam. Follow that dc to the bottom edge of the sleeve. Place a marker there. On the RS of the sleeve, at the bottom edge, attach yarn at the 3rd dc from the left of the center dc that you found.

ROW 1: Ch 3, sk 1st dc, dc in next dc, *ch 1, dc in next dc. Rep from * 2 more times. Dec dc in next 2 dcs. Ch 3, turn.

ROW 2: Sk 1st dc, *dc in next dc, ch 1. Rep from * 1 more time. Dec dc in last 2 dc. Ch 3, turn.

ROW 3: Skip 1st dc. Dec dc in last 2 dc. Ch 1, do not turn.

Repeat these directions on the other sleeve.

Picot Edge

You are working on the RS of the sleeve. Work the picot edge around the sleeve edge, keeping the stitches even and the picot edge flat. Start with a sl st in the next st, *ch 3, sl st in 3rd ch from hk , sk a distance on the sleeve edge, sl st . (1 picot made). Rep from * around. Join with sl st to 1st sl st.

Repeat for the other sleeve.

This project was created with

6 (8, 9) skeins of Schoeller Stahl's *Portofino* in Lemon (#4712), 40% cotton/40% acrylic/20% polyamide, 1.75oz/50g = approx 121yd/110m ea

Copper-Tone Silk Ribbon Tank

Lush and luxuriant are just two of the words you can use to describe this exquisite tank. Yards of hand-dyed silk ribbon caress your bare skin. Go ahead: indulge.

DESIGN BY
Linda Buckner

■ skill level
Experienced

■ finished measurements
This tank is designed to fit bust sizes S (34"/86cm), M (38"/96cm), and L (42"/107cm).

Approx length: (S/M) 21"/53cm, (L) 24"/61cm

■ you will need
Approx 200yd (240, 320)/180m (216, 288) 1½"/4cm wide silk ribbon in copper, deep green/gold, and copper/bright green (approx 50yd per color)

Approx 40yd (40/80)/36m (36, 72) 7⁄16"/1cm wide silk ribbon in copper

Hooks: 15mm/P-Q, 9mm/M/N-13 or sizes needed to obtain gauge

■ stitches used
Chain stitch (ch)

Single rochet (sc)

Triple crochet (tr)

Loop stitch (Lp st)

Alternate loop stitch (Alt Lp st)

■ gauge
Take time to check your gauge.

1.5 stitches = 1"/2.5cm

1 Repeat (Rows 1 & 2) = 3.5"/9cm (approx) with 15mm/P-Q hook.

Pattern Stitches

Loop Stitch (page 22)

Alternate Loop Stitch

Chain desired length, ch 1, turn.

In 3rd ch from hook, make loops approx 2½"- 2¾"/6-7cm in length across to last st, sc In this st. Turn.

ROW 1: Ch 4, pull up loop from previous row to the ch 4 height, insert hook through this loop, yo, pull through, yo, pull through both loops on hook (sc made), continue across to last st, tr in last st, ch 2, turn.

Pattern Notes
The beginning chain counts as a stitch throughout this pattern.

The turning chain may be hard to see with the silk ribbon. Make sure your stitch count is accurate.

Be sure to catch both strands of the loop in loop stitch, the loops will pull out if not caught.

Silk ribbon is slippery to work with, but becomes easier as you get a feel for the material. When joining ribbon lengths or changing colors it's best to tie knots. Woven in ends may have a tendency to pull out. As a last resort, you can tack the ends with sewing thread.

Don't try to keep ribbon loops straight. Measuring each loop is not necessary after the length is first established.

Tank is made in 4 rectangles: sides (2), front center and back center.

Front Center Panel

NOTE: Loops of alternate loop stitch are horizontal on center panels. Center panels are worked side to side.

With 1½"/4cm copper ribbon, ch 25 (25, 31) plus 1. Turn.

In 3rd ch from hk make lp and in each ch across to last ch, sc in last ch. Turn.

Copper-Tone Silk Ribbon Tank

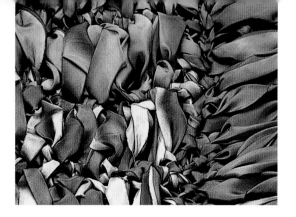

Ch4, Alt Lp st in each lp from prev row, tr in last stitch. Turn.

ROW 1: Ch 2, Lp st in each st across to last st, sc in this st. Turn.

ROW 2: Ch 4, Alt Lp st in each lp of prev row, tr in the last st. Turn.

Rep rows 1 and 2. Fasten off.

Back Center Panel

Note: Worked as for front, but on longer foundation chain.

With 1½"/4cm copper ribbon, ch 30 (30, 36) plus 1. Turn.

Side Panels (make 2)

Front and back sides are made as one vertical panel.

Fasten off each color when joining new colors.

With copper, ch 10 (14, 16) plus1 Turn.

ROW 1: Ch 2, Lp st in each st across to last st, sc in this st. Turn.

ROW 2: Ch 4, Alt Lp st in each lp of prev row, tr in the last st. Turn.

Rep rows 1 and 2 twice.

With copper/bright green, rep rows 1 and 2 twice.

With deep green/gold, rep rows 1 and 2 twice.

With copper, rep rows 1 and 2 twice.

(For Size L only: with copper, rep rows 1 and 2 once.)

With deep green/gold, rep rows 1 and 2 twice.

With copper/bright green, rep rows 1 and 2 twice.

With copper, rep rows 1 and 2 twice. Fasten off.

Finishing

Take care not to catch loops in the seams.

Sew center front and back panels to side panel with 7/16"/1cm ribbon. When sewing the side of the panel with the beginning chain, sew instead to the first row of pattern for a closer seam.

Sew side panels, stopping at the end of copper/bright green section for all sizes (figure 2).

Edging

Crochet over ends for ease in finishing.

With right sides facing using 1½"/4cm deep green/gold ribbon with 9mm/M crochet hook, sc loosely around neck, bottom and armholes.

With right sides facing, using 7/16"/1cm ribbon and 9mm/M hook work back post sc around neck and bottom edge only. Fasten off. Weave in any remaining ends.

This project was created with

2 (2,3) spools of Artemis' *Hannah Silk Ribbon* in Tuscany, 100% silk, 1½"/4cm wide, approx 40yd/36m ea

1 (2,2) spools of Artemis' *Hannah Silk Ribbon* in Fallen Leaves, 100% silk, 1½"/4cm wide, approx 40yd/36m ea

2 (2,3) spools of Artemis' *Hannah Silk Ribbon* in Leaves Turning, 100% silk, 1½"/4cm wide, approx 40yd/36m ea

1 (1,2) spools of Artemis *Hannah Silk Ribbon* in Tuscany, 100% silk, 7/16"/1cm wide, approx 40yd/36m ea

Double Rectangle Top

DESIGN BY
Donna May

This simply constructed top—just two rectangles with a ribbed hem—is a versatile addition to any wardrobe. The bamboo yarn is soft as silk, so you can don the top in warm or cold weather. Give it a truly individual look with an out-of-the-ordinary button of your choice. Go ahead: Splurge on the button. You deserve it!

Double Rectangle Top

finished measurements

The top is designed to fit bust sizes S (34"/86cm), M (38"/96cm), and L (42"/107cm)

Each rectangle for size S measures approx 7 x 26½"/18 x 67cm

you will need

Approx 471yd (562, 795)/424m (506, 716) of DK or light worsted yarn

Hooks: 3.25mm/D-3 for the rectangles, 2.75mm/C for ribbing or sizes needed to obtain gauge

Tapestry needle

1 button, approx 1"/2.5cm diameter

stitches used

Chain stitch (ch)

Double crochet (dc)

Slip Stitch (sl st)

special stitches

Front post double crochet (FPdc): See page 23.

Back post double crochet (BPdc): See page 23.

gauge

Take time to check your gauge.

Rectangles: 18 dc and 10 rows = 4"/10cm.

Ribbing: 6 post sts and 4 rows = 1"/2.5cm

Rectangles (make 2)

Each rectangle approx 7 x 26½" (7¾ x 32, 8¾ x 37)/18 x 67 cm (20 x 81, 22 x 94)

Ch 34 (38, 42).

ROW 1: Dc in 4th ch from hk; dc in ea st across; ch 2, turn. 31 (35, 39) sts. Tie a contrasting color yarn around a st in the first row to mark RS.

ROW 2: Dc in ea st across row; ch 2, turn.

ROWS 3–66 (79, 92: Rep row 2.

ROW 67 (80, 93): Dc in ea st across row. Fasten off. Weave in ends.

Assembling Rectangles

With WS together, fold each rectangle in half, matching edges of short sides. The fold creates the top of the shoulder and cap sleeve. Pin side seams along approx 6" (7, 9)/15cm (18, 23) from lower edge. Thread a tapestry needle with matching yarn and sew side seams with a back stitch. Weave in ends.

Front: With RS facing, lap the right lower front edge over the left lower front edge by two 2½" (3, 3½)/5cm (8, 8). Pin together. Baste with yarn approx ½"/1cm from edge and remove pins. (Sew long running stitches across overlap to baste; you will remove these stitches later.)

Back: In same manner as for the front, with right side facing, again overlap by 2½"(3, 3½)/5cm (8, 8). Pin together, baste, and remove pins.

Ribbing

Approx 2" (2½, 3)/5cm (5, 8) wide

Ribbing is worked in the round with size 2.75mm/C-2 hook. Do not turn your work at the end of the rounds.

RND 1: With RS facing, attach yarn in a side seam at lower edge and ch 1. Inserting hk between dc sts in prev row, sc evenly around (taking care to crochet through both layers at overlaps); join with a sl st in beg ch st; ch 2. Tie a contrasting color of yarn around the ch 2 to mark end of rnd.

RND 2: Dc in next st and cont dc in each st around, making 1 (2, 3) dec dc at ea side and 1 (1, 1) dec dc at ea overlap; join with sl st in top ch of ch 2; ch 2. [4 (6, 8) dec made.]

RND 3: *BPdc around first dc, FPdc around next dc; repeat from * around, ending with sl st in top ch of ch 2 to join; ch 2.

RND 4 TO END: *BPdc around next BPdc, FPdc around next FPdc; rep from * to end of round; ending with sl st in top ch of ch-2 to join; ch 2. When a ribbing width of 2"(2½, 3)/5cm (6, 8) is reached, sl st at end of round in top ch of ch 2 to join; fasten off and weave in ends.

Remove basting stitches.

Finishing

Sew button on 3rd dc from center edge on left side. Suggested placement: 7"(8, 9)/18cm (20, 23) up from ribbing on left front. Adjust placement to suit bust measurement and desired neckline depth.

Slip button between 2 dc stitches directly across, in same row on right front to fasten.

You may create an optional button loop for use with larger button. Crochet a chain twice the diameter of your button and leave a 7"/18cm tail of yarn. Loop chain over button to determine appropriate location on the right front to sew loop. Thread the tail of the chain in a tapestry needle and sew both ends of chain to wrong side of right front of top. Pull loop up through to the right side.

Fitting Note

Though the fit can be fine tuned by changing placement of button, if narrower shoulders are required in the garment, the spread of the shoulders can be reduced by tacking down a section of the back overlap using a yarn-threaded tapestry needle. To do this, work on wrong side and pick up surface loops of stitches so the stitching will be invisible on the right side of the top. Sew the overlap together for a length of 1"/2.5cm or more up from ribbing.

This project was created with

2 (3, 4) balls Southwest Trading's 100% *Bamboo Yarn* in Turquoise Green/Jade, 3.5oz/100g = approx 250yd/225m ea

Snuggly Azure Shrug

Imagine wrapping yourself in a puffy cloud snatched from out of the blue: soft, light, yet capable of warding off the chill of an early spring day.

DESIGN BY
Donna May

■ skill level
Easy

■ finished measurements
Finished rectangle measures approx 30 x 55"/76 x 140cm

One size fits most

■ you will need
783yd/704m fancy worsted weight yarn*

Hook: 9mm/M/N-13 or size needed to obtain gauge

Tapestry needle

Elastic thread (optional)

For a thicker fabric (and even more snuggly shrug), work two strands of yarn together throughout (1566 yd/1408m).

■ stitches used
Chain stitch (ch)

Half double crochet (hdc)

■ gauge
Take time to check your gauge.

Approx 8 st = 4"/10cm

7 rows = 4"/10cm

Pattern Notes
Hdc is worked in first stitch at beginning of row throughout. After starting a new ball of yarn, weave in ends before continuing.

Pattern

Ch 99 and make 1 hdc in 3rd ch from hk and in ea ch across; ch 2, turn (96 sts).

ROWS 1–4: Hdc across; ch 2, turn. Tie a short piece of contrasting color yarn around a st in first row to mark RS.

ROW 5: 1 hdc in first 46 hdc; 2 dec hdc, 1 hdc in ea of next 46 hdc; ch 2, turn (94 sts).

ROW 6: 1 hdc in first 44 hdc; 3 dec hdc, 1 hdc in ea of next 44 hdc; ch 2, turn. (91 sts)

ROWS 7–58: Hdc in each hdc across; ch 2, turn. (91 sts)

ROW 59: Hdc in each of first 44 hdc; 3 inc hdc; 1 hdc in ea of next 44 hdc; ch 2, turn. (94 sts)

ROW 60: Hdc in each of first 46 hdc; 2 inc hdc; 1 hdc in ea of next 46 hdc; ch 2, turn. (96 sts)

ROWS 61–64: Hdc in each hdc across (96 sts); fasten off. Weave in ends.

Assembly

Sleeve Seams
With right sides together, fold piece in half lengthwise, bringing top edge to foundation chain edge (figure 1 on page 122). Mark off 14"/36 cm on each end where edges meet (long edge). Back stitch edges of one 14"/36cm section together to create sleeve seam. Fasten off. Weave in ends. Repeat with other section.

Optional Sleeve Length
To extend sleeves to wrist length attach yarn now to right side of the fabric at the cuff and crochet around cuff edge in hdc. Continue crocheting in the round until sleeve is desired length.

Snuggly Azure Shrug

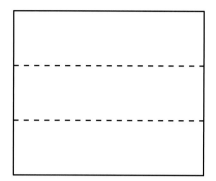

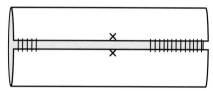

Figure 1

(Do not ch 2 at beginning of each round; simply make the first hdc of round 2 and later rounds into the first stitch of the last round.) When sleeve is desired length, join, fasten off and weave in ends.

Gathering Cuffs

Thread about a 40"/102cm length of yarn or elastic thread in needle and fasten to WS of one sleeve seam at cuff edge. Make a running stitch near edge, around circumference of sleeve opening. Pull to gather cuff to 5½"/14cm diameter opening. Check before fastening to be sure there is enough stretch to allow the hand through the opening, as elasticity may vary in different threads. Fasten off. Weave in end. Repeat for other cuff.

Finishing

This section is crocheted in the round. You will crochet in each stitch; however, in half the round, you will crochet into hdc stitches and the other half of the round you will crochet into the free loops of your foundation chain. No stitch count is necessary for these rounds and is not provided, as the number will vary slightly with number of stitches sewn in the sleeve sections.

With RS facing you, fasten yarn in one inner sleeve seam at armhole opening and ch 2. (Tie a contrasting color yarn in this stitch to mark the beginning of the round.)

RND 1: Inc hdc in ea st around. Sl st in top ch of beginning ch 2 to join; ch 2, turn.

RNDS 2–3: Hdc in 1st st and in ea st around. Sl st in top ch of ch-2 to join, ch 2, turn.

RND 4: Hdc in ea st around. Sl st in top ch of ch 2 to join. Fasten off. Weave in ends.

Forming Collar

Lay the shrug flat with sleeve seams facing you and centered half way between top and bottom edges of sleeves. (It doesn't matter which side you use for the top of the shrug.) Create collar by folding back the middle section of the open center edge. The collar will fold back naturally due to the stitching, however, the width may adjusted as desired.

If desired, tack down collar by catching several stitches along the back of the collar and sewing to the shrug body directly underneath. Catch only bottom loops of back of collar to avoid stitches showing on top.

Not Your Granny's Halter Top

These "Friendship Squares" start new friendships all 'round. When you step out in this fun, retro-style halter top, crocheters will want to know how-to, and others will just want know: Who's the girl in the groovy top?

DESIGN BY
Gwen Blakley Kinsler

Not Your Granny's Halter Top

■ **skill level**

Beginner

■ **finished measurements**

Approx 5 x 5"/13 x 13 cm each square

The top is designed to fit bust sizes S (34"/86cm), M (38"/96cm), and L (42"/107cm)

■ **you will need**

Yarn A: 330yd/306m cotton/nylon worsted weight ribbon in green

Yarn B: 110yd/102m cotton/nylon worsted weight ribbon in plum

Yarn C: 220yd/204m cotton/nylon worsted weight ribbon in variegated green/blue

Hook: 4mm/G-6 or size needed to obtain gauge

Approx 80 pony beads

Sewing needle and matching thread

Tapestry needle

■ **stitches used**

Chain stitch (ch)

Single crochet (sc)

Double crochet (dc)

Reverse single crochet (rev sc)

2 double crochet cluster (2-dc cl)

3 double crochet cluster (3-dc cl)

Pattern Notes

Color Combinations

Color Combo 1: 2 rnds of yarn A, 1 rnd each of yarns B, C, A
Color Combo 2: 2 rnds of yarn C, 1 rnd each of yarns A, C, A
Color Combo 3: 2 rnds of yarn B, 1 rnd each of yarns A, C, A

Squares Needed per Size

Small = 12 squares: 6 of combo 2, 3 ea of combo 3 and 1
Medium = 14 squares: 7 of combo 2, 3 of combo 3, 4 of combo 1
Large = 16 squares: 4 ea of combo 1 and 3, 8 of combo 2

Friendship Square

Ch 4, sl st to form ring.

RND 1: Work 8 sc in ring; join with sl st to first sc. Do not turn.

RND 2: Ch 3, work dc in same place as sl st, ch 2, *yo hook, draw up lp in next sc, yo, draw through 2 lps on hk, yo, draw up lp in same stitch, yo, draw through 2 lps on hk, yo draw through remaining 3 lps on hk (2-dc cl made), ch 2; rep from * 6 times; join with sl st to top of ch 3 (eight 2-dc cl, counting ch 3 as 1 dc). Fasten off.

RND 3: With next yarn color, sl st in any ch-2 sp, ch 3, work 2-dc cl in same sp, ch 3, (yo, draw up lp in same space, yo, draw through 2 lps on hk) 3 times, yo, draw through remaining 4 lps on hk (3-dc cl made: 1stcorner), * ch 2, work 3-dc cl in next ch-2 sp, ch 2, work 3-dc cl, ch 3 and 3-dc cl in next ch-2 sp (another corner complete). Rep from * twice; ch 2, 3-dc cl in next sp; join with sl st. Fasten off.

RND 4: With next yarn color, sl st in any corner ch-3 sp, work 1st corner in same sp, *(ch 2, work 3-dc cl in next ch-2 sp) twice; ch 2, work corner in next ch-2 sp. Rep from * twice; (ch 2, work 3-dc cl in next ch-2 sp) twice; ch 2; join. Fasten off.

RND 5: With next yarn color, sl st in any corner ch-3 sp; work 1st corner in same sp, * (2, work 3 dc cl in next ch-2 sp) 3 times; ch 2, work corner in next ch-3 sp. Rep from * twice; (ch 2, work 3-dc cl in next ch-2 sp) 3 times; ch 2; join with sl st. Fasten off. Weave in ends.

Joining Squares

Lay squares in sequences as follows:

Small

Row 1 of Squares: combo 2, 3, 2, 3, 2, 3
Row 2 of Squares: combo 1, 2, 1, 2, 1, 2

Medium

Row 1 of Squares: combo 1, 2, 1, 2, 1, 2, 1
Row 2 of Squares: combo 2, 3, 2, 3, 2, 3, 2

Large

Row 1 of Squares: combo 2, 1, 2, 1, 2, 1, 2, 1
Row 2 of Squares: combo 3, 2, 3, 2, 3, 2, 3, 2

Join squares with yarn A. Sl st, holding RS together and matching stitches on the outer edges.

Insert the hook under the outside loop (loop closest to you) on the front piece and under the corresponding outside loop (loop furthest away from you) on the back piece.

Repeat this process for each stitch from 2nd ch in corner to 2nd ch in next corner.

When squares of each row are joined, join 2 rows together.

Finally, join side seam in same way.

Top Edging

With front of halter facing, using yarn A, sc evenly around entire top edge; do not fasten off; ch 1, work rev sc in each sc just worked. Fasten off.

Bottom Edging

With front of halter facing, sl st to join to any stitch at side. Ch 3, sk 1 stitch, hdc in next st, *ch 1, sk 1 stitch, hdc in next stitch; repeat from * around; join with sl st in 2nd ch of ch 3. With yarn A, make a chain of approx 44" (49, 54)/112cm (124, 137) and weave through ch-1 spaces at lower edge of halter.

Straps (make 2)

With yarn A, ch 100 (110, 120), leaving a tail of approx 4"/10cm on each end of ch. Repeat with yarns B and C. Knot 3 strands together and braid them; knot on other end. Repeat for 2nd strap.

Sew these straps to halter approx 2 1/2"/6cm in from side seam on both front and back.

Fringe

Cut 25"/64cm lengths of all three colors of yarn. Attach them with overhand knot to bottom edge of halter, alternating colors. Attach 3 beads to ends of yarn A fringe and knot the fringe to hold the beads. More beads can be attached if desired.

This project was created with

Berroco's *Zen* in Kimchi (#8222), 3 balls; Umeboshi (#8244), 1 ball; Osaka Mix (#8139), 2 balls, 40% cotton/60% nylon, 1.75oz/50g = approx 110yd/102m ea

Silk Meringue Bolero

DESIGN BY
Linda Buckner

This confection of a bolero is as scrumptious as the topping on a lemon meringue pie. Light and fluffy with just a hint of sweetness, it's the perfect topping for a special occasion's little black dress or perhaps a pair of slinky jeans and a silken wisp of a top.

Pattern Notes

Silk ribbon is slippery to work with, but it becomes easier as you get a feel for the material. Fasten off as you change ribbon. When joining ribbon lengths, it's best to tie knots. Woven in ends have a tendency to pull out. As a last resort, you can tack the ends with sewing thread.

Do not try to keep ribbon loops straight. Measuring each loop is not necessary after the length is first established.

The bolero body is made in one piece to the armholes. Consistency is easier if fronts and back are worked across using three separate spools/yarn from the armholes to the neck.

The turning chain counts as a stitch throughout the pattern. The chain will be difficult to see with the silk. Take care to keep your stitch count accurate.

Be sure to catch both strands of the loop in the loop stitch: The loops will pull out if not caught.

Increases are made on the loop rows, decreases on the return rows.

Directions are written for size S (M, L).

Bolero body

With 10mm/N/P-15 hk and 1½"/4cm ribbon, ch 60 (68, 76) plus 1. Turn. [13 (16,19) sts for ea front, 34 (36,38) sts for back.]

ROW 1: Make beg Lp st in the 3rd chain from the hk, and in ea ch across to the last ch, sc in last ch. Ch 2, turn.

ROW 2: Sc in ea st across. Tie on one strand mohair and one strand 7/16"/1cm ribbon (held together throughout), ch 2, turn.

[Size L only: Rep rows 1 and 2 (ch 2 to begin row 1) once more.]

ROW 3: Make a Lp st in the same space as the chain (inc made), Lp st across to last st, 2 sc in the last st (inc made). Ch 3, Turn. [15 (18, 21) sts ea front, 38 (40, 42) sts back]

ROW 4: Hdc in ea stitch across. Turn.

Row 5: Change to 1½"/4cm ribbon, ch 2, make Lp st in same space (inc made), Lp st across to the last st, make Lp st and sc in last stitch (inc made). Ch 2, Turn. [17 (20, 23) sts ea front, 42 (44, 46) sts back]

ROW 6: Sc in ea stitch across. Turn.

ROW 7: Change to mohair and 7/16"/1cm ribbon, ch 2, Lp st in same space (inc made), Lp st across to last stitch, one Lp st and one sc in last stitch (inc made). Ch 3, turn. [19 (22,25) sts each front, 46 (48, 50) sts back]

Silk Meringue Bolero

■ special stitches

Loop stitch (see page 22)

Alternate Loop Stitch

Chain desired length, ch 1, turn.

In 3rd ch from hook, make loops approx 2¹⁄2"- 2³⁄4"/6-7cm in length across to last st, sc In this st. Turn.

Row 1: Ch 4, pull up loop from previous row to the ch 4 height, insert hook through this loop, yo, pull through, yo, pull through both loops on hook (sc made), continue across to last st, tr in last st, ch 2, turn.

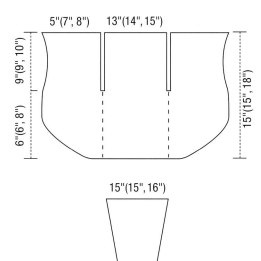

ROW 8: Dc in ea st across. Ch 2, turn.

Divide for armholes

ROW 9: (For the front) with 1½"/4cm ribbon Lp st across, sc in 19th (22, 25) st; (for the back) tie on new spool, ch 2, Lp st across with sc in 34th (36, 38) st; (for the front) tie on new spool, ch 2, Lp st across, sc in last st. Turn.

ROW 10: Tie on mohair and ⁷⁄16"/1cm ribbon. Begin decrease row: (For the front) Ch 2, yo draw up loop, draw up loop in next st, yo and take off 3 loops, yo and take off remaining 2 loops (dec made), dc across, dec in last 2 sts. (For the back) Ch 2, dc dec., dc across, Dc dec. (For the front) ch 2, dc dec., dc across, dc dec. Turn.

ROW 11: (For fronts and back): Change to 1"/2.5cm ribbon, ch 2, Lp st across, sc in last st. Turn.

ROW 12: (For the front) ch 2, sc dec, sc across; (For the back) ch 2, sc dec, sc across, sc dec; (For the front) ch 2, sc across, sc dec. Turn.

ROW 13: (For fronts and back): With mohair and ⁷⁄16"/1cm ribbon, ch 2, Lp st across, sc in last st ea front and back. Turn.

ROW 14: (For the front) ch 3, dc dec, dc across; (For the back) ch 3, dc across (no dec); (For the front) ch 3, dc across, dc dec. Turn.

Continue to alternate 1"/2.5cm ribbon (sc return rows) with mohair and ⁷⁄16"/1cm ribbon (dc return rows) as established until there are 10 (11,12) sts remaining ea front. (Back is worked even, no further decs) End with a mohair/⁷⁄16th"/1cm ribbon Lp st row or 1"/2.5cm Lp st row (size dependent). Fasten off.

Sleeves (make 2)

With 1½"/4cm ribbon, ch 16 (16,18) plus 1, turn.

ROW 1: In the 2nd ch from hk, make Lp st and in ea ch across to last ch, sc. Turn. [You will have ch2, 14 (14,16) Lp sts, 1 sc= 16 (16,18) sts]

ROW 2: Ch 4, work Alt lp st across to last st, tr in last stitch. Turn.

ROW 3: Change to mohair and ⁷⁄16th"/1cm ribbon, ch 2, Lp st across, sc in last st. Turn.

ROW 4: Ch 2, sc in the same space, sc across, 2 sc in last st. Turn. [18 (18, 20) sts]

ROW 5: With 1½"/4cm ribbon, ch 2, Lp st across, sc. Turn.

ROW 6: Ch 2, sc in same sp, sc across, 2 sc in last st. Turn. [20 (20, 22) sts]

ROW 7: Rep row 3.

ROW 8: Rep row 4 [22 (22, 24) sts]

Continue rep rows alternating 1½"/4cm ribbon and mohair with ⁷/₁₆th"/1cm ribbon and mohair, incs until there are 26 (26, 28) sts.

NEXT ROW: Change to 1"/2.5cm ribbon, ch 2, Lp st across, sc.

RETURN ROW: Inc to 28 (28, 30) sts

LAST ROW: With mohair and ⁷/₁₆"/1cm ribbon, ch 2, Lp st across, sc. Fasten off.

Finishing

Please note: This fabric has a good amount of give.

With ⁷/₁₆"/1cm ribbon and mohair together, sew shoulder seams, being careful not to catch loops in seam. Sew sleeve seams. Inset sleeves and sew. (Sewing with one strand of either ribbon or mohair alone is not secure enough).

If needed, steam on the wrong side (do not place iron directly on stitches). Dry clean only.

Edging

With ⁷/₁₆"/1cm ribbon and mohair using 9mm/M-N 13 hk, begin at an underarm seam of the bottom and ch 2, sc around (crochet over ends to simplify finishing) bottom, sides and neck edges, ending with a sl st to beginning ch2. (No edging is necessary on the sleeves).

Optional Embellishments

Couch prestrung pearls, beads, or even rhinestones around all edges.

Couch fur or lace around neck, front, and sleeve edges.

Loops can be cut and will resemble fringe.

This project was created with

5 (5, 6) spools of Artemis' *Hannah Silk* in Bridal Ivory, 100% silk, 1½"/4cm wide, ea spool approx 40yd/36m

3 (3, 4) spools of Artemis' *Hannah Silk* in Bridal Ivory, 100% silk, 1"/2.5cm wide, ea spool approx 40yd/36m

6 (6,7) spools of Artemis' *Hannah Silk* in Bridal Ivory, 100% silk, ⁷/₁₆"/1cm wide , ea spool approx 40yd/36m

2 skeins of Mountain Colors' *Mohair* in Natural, 78% mohair/13% wool/9% nylon, 3.5oz/100g = approx 225yd/203m ea

Reversible Halter and Scarf

DESIGN BY
Ruthie Marks

You'll need to pay a bit more attention when you crochet this top, but the result is well worth the effort. If your skill level isn't top-notch, the scarf is a delightful project.

Pattern Notes

This is a double-sided garment. No ends are fastened off until each section is completed.

Use an overhand knot at the end of each row to keep stitches from unraveling while you work.

If you find that the 2 stitches you're picking up are not in alignment, chances are you have picked up an extra stitch or dropped one along the way. Count your stitches often.

When you lay down your work, have both working threads at the same end; this tells you that yarn A begins the next row.

Back

Row 1: With yarn A and 6.5mm/K-10½ hk, ch 50 (54, 58), sc in 2nd ch from hk and each ch across, turn [49 (53, 57) sts].

ROW 2A: Ch 1, sc in front loop of each sc across, drop A, do not turn.

ROW 2B: With B, go back to beg of row 2A and, *inserting the hk from the top down, sc in the back lp of the 1st stitch of row 2A and the free lp of the 1st stitch of row 1, rep in the 2nd st and each st across, drop B, pick up A.

ROW 3A: With A, ch 1, turn and, *inserting the hk from the top down, sc in the back lp of B and the free lp of A, rep from * across, drop A, pick up B.

ROW 3B: With B, ch 1, turn and, *inserting the hk from the bottom up, sc in the free lp of B and the front lp of A, rep from * across, drop B, pick up A.

ROW 4A: With A, ch 1, turn and, *inserting the hook from the bottom up, sc in the free lp of A and the front lp of B, repeat from * across, drop A, pick up B.

ROW 4B: With B, ch 1, turn and, *inserting the hk from the top down, sc in the back lp of A and the free lp of B, repeat from * across, drop B, pick up A.

The pattern is a repeat of rows 3A, 3B, 4A, 4B.

Work in pattern stitch until approx 9 (9, 10)"/23(23, 25)cm from beginning. At the end of last 2 rows fasten off A and B.

Front

Work as back to 9(9, 10)" /23(23, 25)cm from beg.

ROW 1A: (beg dec): Sk 1st 2 sts of B, with A sl st in first 2 sts of A,

■ **skill level**

Top: Experienced

Scarf: Easy

■ **finished measurements**

Top: S (29"/74cm), M (31"/79cm), L (33"/84cm) *

Scarf: approx 8 x 54"/20 x 137cm (excluding fringe)

The fabric of this garment, because it is worked loosely, is very stretchy, so dimensions are smaller than standard sizing.

■ **you will need**

Yarn A: approx 460yd (544, 628)/414m (490, 565) of fine/sport weight yarn in orange

Yarn B: 376yd (460, 544)/338m (414, 490) of fine/sport weight yarn in pale green

Hooks: 6.5mm/K/10½, 6mm/J/10, 5.5mm/I-9, 3.5mm/E-4 or sizes needed to obtain gauge

Tapestry needle

20"/51cm 3mm elastic thread

■ **stitches used**

Chain stitch (ch)

Single crochet (sc)

Half double crochet (hdc)

Double crochet (dc)

■ **gauge**

Take time to check your gauge.

Top: 14 st = 4"/10cm
12 rows = 4"/10cm

Scarf: 6 arches = 4"/10cm
14 rows = 4"/10cm

Reversible Halter and Scarf

(sl st, ch 1, sc in A and B) in next st, work in pattern in next 45 sts, leave last 2 sts unworked [45 (49, 53) sts]

ROW 1B: With B, work same as 1A.

ROW 2A: Sk 1st st of B, with A sl st in first st of A, (sl st, ch 1, sc in A and B) in next st, work in pattern in next 43 sts, leave last st unworked. [43 (47, 51) sts]

ROW 2B: With B, work same as 2A.

ROW 3A: With A, ch 1 and work even across.

ROW 3B: With B, work same as 3A.

ROWS 4A AND 4B: Rep row 2A and 2B. [41 (45, 49) sts]

ROWS 5A AND 5B: Rep row 2A and 2B [39 (43, 47)sts]

ROWS 6A AND 6B: Rep row 3A and 3B [29 (43, 47) sts]

Repeat rows 4A–6B for approx 5"(6, 6)/13cm (15, 15) from beg of dec. [31 (27, 27) sts]. Fasten off A and B.

Joining Side Seams (2 each for A and B)
With side A facing, use a strand of yarn A and a tapestry needle to sew both side A edges together.

With side B facing, use a strand of yarn B and a tapestry needle to sew both side B edges together.

Casing (across top of front)
ROW 1: With side B facing, 5.5mm/I-9 hook and 2 strands of A, attach with 1 sc in first st and sc across, turn [31 (27, 27) sts].

ROW 2: Ch 3 (counts as hdc and ch 1), sk first 2 sc, hdc in next sc, *ch 1, sk 1 sc, hdc in next sc, repeat from * across, fasten off.

Edging Around Top Edges
Starting at side seam with side B facing, 5.5mm/ I-9 hook and 2 strands of A, going through both loops of both B and A, matching stitch for stitch, (sl st, ch 1) in each st across back and up side, (sl st, ch 1) in each hdc only across top, (sl st, ch 1) in each st down other side, sl st to beg sl st, fasten off.

Bottom Edging
RND 1: With side B facing, 5.5mm/I-9 hook and 2 strands of A, join with sl st at side seam. Working in sps between sts, *sk 2

spaces, 5 dc in next sp, skip 2 sps, sl st in next sp, repeat from *
around, ending sl st in beg sl st, turn.

RND 2: *5 dc in middle dc of dc group in rnd 1, sl st in next sl st,
rep from * around, ending sl st in beg sl st, fasten off.

Neck Cord

With 5.5mm/I-9 hook and 2 strands of A, ch 170, fasten off
(approx 40"/102cm). Tie a knot in end and trim ends to
1"/2.5cm. Thread through row of hdc at top of halter and tie in a
bow behind the neck.

Finishing

If desired, thread tapestry needle with elastic thread. Weave
thread through edging across back of garment and adjust to cus-
tomize fit. Secure ends.

Scarf

Side A

ROW 1: With yarn A and 3.5mm/E-4 hk, ch 302, sc in 6th ch from
hk, *ch 5, sk 3ch, sc in next ch, rep from * to end, turn.

ROWS 2–14: Ch 5, sc in next ch-5 arch, rep from * to end, turn.
Fasten off at the end of row 14.

Side B

ROW 1 (RS): Working across the other side of the foundation row,
join B with sc in the first ch, *ch 5, sc opposite the next sc, rep
from * to end, turn.

ROWS 2–14: Rep rows 2–14 of side A.

Fringe

Using an 8"/20cm wide piece of cardboard, wind and cut 48
strands each of A and B. Work with groups of 6, attach in beginning ch-5 loops of 4 rows at each end of scarf. Trim ends evenly.

This project was created with

2 skeins ea of Red Heart's *Luster
Sheen* in Persimmon (#257) and Tea
Leaf (#615), 100% acrylic, 4oz/113g
= approx 335 yds/306 m ea

Lady of the Baskervilles Vest

The houndstooth pattern of this vest should give you a clue, Sherlock. This contemporary take on a traditional pattern will certainly make any and all witnesses take notice. Can you picture sleuthing about the fog-shrouded moors in this? How about attending an autumn tailgate party on a brilliant Saturday afternoon?

DESIGN BY
Paula Gron

■ **skill level**
Experienced

■ **finished measurements**
This vest is designed to fit bust sizes S (34"/86cm), M (38"/96cm), and L (42"/107cm)

■ **you will need**
Yarn A: approx 390yd/355m 100% wool bulky yarn in off-white

Yarn B: approx 390yd/355m 100% wool bulky yarn in charcoal

Hook: 6.5mm/ K–10½

Tapestry needle

■ **stitches used**
Chain stitch (ch)

Single crochet (sc)

Loop stitch (Lp st)

■ **gauge**
Take time to check your gauge.

9 sts = 4"/10cm

8.5 rows = 4"/10cm

Pattern Notes

The vest is made in three pieces: a back and two fronts. Pockets are made separately.

Read chart in the direction the crochet is worked from the bottom to top, left to right (WS) and right to left (RS) when working in rows.

Follow the charts for color and yarn changes. Each square represents a stitch and each horizontal line represents a row. Always introduce the next color in the final yarn over (yo) of the previous sitch. This includes when the color change is needed in the turning stitch from row to row. The color not in use is carried along the top of the previous row and stitched over.

Carry yarn temporarily not in use loosely across top of the previous row so as to hide and not distort (see page 000). Take care to keep color changes neat. Fasten off yarn B before doing those rows stitch only in yarn A and join again for next row.

The turning chain counts as a stitch throughout.

Color Work Notes

1. Always introduce the second color in the final yo of the previous stitch. This includes when color change is needed in the turning stitch from row to row. The base color (in this case the cream) is then carried along the top of the previous row.

2. The two yarns exchange roles when the base color is required again.

The base color is NOT introduced in final yo of previous stitch, it is just exchanged and worked. This creates the diagonal point of the houndstooth check.

Shaping Notes

When increasing or decreasing a single stitch on the beginning or end of a row, either sc twice into the stitch or sc decrease.

To decrease more than 1 stitch at the beginning of a row, sl st back over the previous row the required number of stitches, ch 1 (counts as a stitch) and continue across the row.

Lady of the Baskervilles Vest

To increase more than 1 stitch at either the beginning or end of a row, chain the number of stitches to increase plus 1, turn and stitch into the 2nd chain from the hook and continue.

Work back shoulders separately after splitting for neck.

Houndstooth Pattern

(starting at bottom of back). Follow chart for subsequent rows.

ROW 1 (RS): With yarn A, ch 43 (45,47), turn. Sc in 2nd ch from hook. Sc in each rem ch across. Add yarn B in yo of last stitch, turn. 42(44,46 sc)

ROW 2 (WS): Following chart, with yarn B, ch 1. Switch to yarn A and sc in next 4 sc, *with yarn B sc in next sc, with yarn A sc in next 4 sc; rep from * across row to last 2 sc, with yarn B sc in next sc and switch to yarn A for last sc stitch. Add yarn B in yo of last stitch, turn.

ROW 3 (RS): Ch 1, with yarn B sc in first 2 sc, with yarn A sc in next 2 sc, *with yarn B sc in next 3 sc, with yarn A sc in next 2 sc; rep from * across Row to last 2 sc, with yarn B sc in last 2 sc, turn.

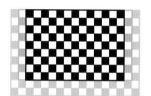

black = small

orange = medium

green = large

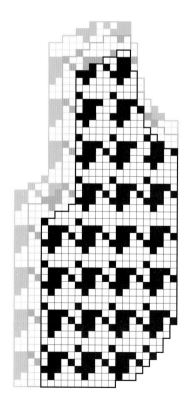

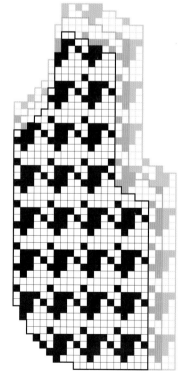

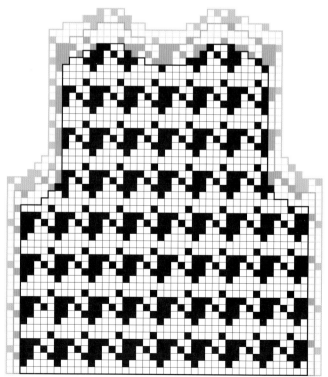

ROW 4 (WS): Ch 1, with yarn B sc in next sc, *with yarn A sc in next 1 sc, with yarn B sc in next 1 sc, with yarn A sc in next 1 sc, with yarn B sc in next 2 sc. Repeat from *to end of row, turn.

ROW 5 (RS): Ch 1, with yarn B sc in next 2 sc, *with yarn A sc in next 2 sc, with yarn B sc in next 3 sc. Repeat from * to end of row, turn.

ROW 6 (WS): With yarn A ch 1, sc in next 3 sc, with yarn B sc in next 1 sc, *with yarn A sc in next 4 sc, with yarn B sc in next 1 sc. Repeat from * to last 2 sc. With yarn A sc in last 2 sc, turn. Break off 3″ tail of yarn B. Continue with yarn A only.

ROW 7 (RS): Ch 1, sc in each sc across to end of row. Add yarn B in yo of last st, turn. 42 (44,46 sc)

Follow chart to make the back, right front, and left front (figure 3).

Pockets (make 2)

Following the pocket chart (figure 4), work from bottom to top for both pockets. Left to right (WS) and right to left (RS). Make color changes for check pattern in the same way as before. Use yarn B for turning chains throughout, counted as the first stitch of every row.

Using yarn A, ch 14 (16, 18), turn. Follow the pocket chart for the appropriate size.

Finish on all sizes with yarn A only (RS), ch 1 and sl st across row. Fasten off.

Finishing

Block each piece.

Because of the weight of each piece, assemble by sewing seams together with back stitching. With yarn A only, sew seams close to pattern edges. Start at shoulder seam. With tapestry needle, work loose ends of yarn B at seam lines back into the seam to hide. Back stitch side seams of front to back in the same way. After stitching, block all seams.

Pocket Assembly

NOTE: Stitches are best completed by catching threads on the vest that lie parallel to the pockets' edges. Fasten off in last stitch.

Lady of the Baskervilles Vest

With final row at top, center each pocket on front pieces. Align bottom edge of pocket to the top of the 6th row from bottom edge of each front piece. Pin securely in place all around.

To make loop stitch, you may need to fold the fabric of the vest back as you catch stitches from the vest to the pocket. Work 1 sc before beginning loop stitches.

Secure pocket to vest with Lp st, working from top right edge, across bottom (right to left) and back up to top left edge of pocket. With yarn A, work approximately 33 Lp sts around each pocket.

Finishing Edges

With yarn A, sc around armhole openings. Sc over loose ends of yarn B as you stitch. Take about 60 sts around per armhole (1 st per side of row works best). Join with sl st to first ch lp. Fasten off.

For finishing front edges, with yarn B, sc down the straight center edge of each front piece for about 18 sts or to row 20 from the bottom edge. Work from top down on left front edge. Fasten off. Work from bottom up on right front edge. Fasten off.

Fringe

NOTE: All remaining loop stitches on vest edges are worked from the inside of the vest.

The loose yarn B strands left hanging from the pattern can be left as added fringe.

Work 1 sc before beginning loop stitches.

For neckline fringe, attach yarn B at left front of neckline, pulling up a lp, work 1 sc and 22 Lp sts at edge up to shoulder seam. Work another 18 Lp sts at back edge to next shoulder seam and 22 more Lp sts to end at right front of neckline. (62 Lp sts)

For bottom edge fringe, attach yarn B at inside of right front at last yarn B ch (approx row 20 from the bottom). Work 1 sc and 37 (39,41) Lp sts at edge to first side seam. Work another 42 Lp sts across back bottom edge to opposite side seam and 37 (39, 41) Lp sts up edge to right front. Total 116 (120, 124) Lp sts.

With scissors, cut loops even on fringe of entire vest, including pockets. If you prefer a feathered appearance, use a fine steel comb or pet brush to feather the fringe.

Buttons and Buttonhole Loops

Apply tighter tension throughout for creating buttons and ch closures.

Buttons (make 6)

With yarn A, create slip knot to begin ch with a 6"/15cm tail. Ch 7 and join with sl st to make loop. Ch 1, 10 sc around ring catching some of tail in but not hiding completely. Join with sl st to first sc and sl st into every other sc (5). Draw yarn through last sc and cut off approx 3"/8cm to fasten off. Draw strand through hole to back side (obvious ring side) to create yarn floret button.

Be sure that 1 strand lies opposite the other strand on ring edge. Use tapestry needle to sew the pulled-through strand to opposite edge if needed.

Attach buttons to vest about approx 1–2"/2.5–5cm from unfringed front edges, 3 per side.

With tapestry needle, sew strands into vest and secure with square knot on inside. Hide yarn ends within pattern.

Buttonhole Loops (make 3)

With yarn B, ch 30. Sl st to first ch. Pull loop through leaving approx 6"/15cm and fasten off.

Place each loop around buttons on right side with end strands, sew each loop into vest front as near as possible to button on right side. Secure with square knot on inside. Use tapestry needle to sew 6"/15cm strand from front to back of vest around the two chs near button. Stitch several times and hide yarn ends inside.

This project was created with

5 skeins Patons' *UpCountry* in Soft Cream (#80906), 100% wool, 3½oz/100g = approx 78yd/71m ea

5 skeins Patons' *UpCountry* in Charcoal (#80996), 100% wool, 3½oz/100g = approx 78yd/71m ea

Designer Biographies

Linda Buckner is an award-winning fiber artist from Wheaton, Illinois. She utilizes high quality fibers in "luscious" colors, felt, fabric, antique embellishments, wire and more to create visually stunning art to wear, collages, home décor, and gift items. She creates new products for a toy manufacturer, teaches, and exhibits mixed media art nationally.

Paula Gron lives with her sculptor husband, Jack, and their cat in the high desert of Flagstaff, Arizona. Her first craft project—at age 8—was a saddle she made out of newspaper and rope for a bronco-busting seat on a porch railing. She is an award-winning graphic designer and commercial illustrator, and has now combined her design background with her love of crafting.

Jennifer Hansen lives in Fremont, California. Though her background is in architecture and computer application architecture, she treats her design and construction of crochet as a problem of material, form, and structure. Her self-published designs have been well received. Visit her website at www.stitchdiva.com to view more of her designs.

Donna Hulka is a former Marylander now living in beautiful North Carolina with her husband and Golden Retriever. She has been making crafts of all kinds all her life and learned to crochet when she was a young girl. She is grateful to the many folks along the way who have taught, inspired, and encouraged her to craft.

Kalpna Kapoor has been crocheting since she was ten years old. She teaches both knitting and crochet workshops and owns Craft-Creations Knitting Studios in Newhall, California. This full-service retail store offers a full range of knitting and crochet classes, as well as a wide selection of fine yarns from around the world.

Robyn Kelly lives in Ventura, California. Her sister Amber, nieces, and her goddaughter are inspirations (and recipients!) of her creative crochet. Like many, her grandmother taught her to crochet at an early age, but she considers herself self-taught.

Gwen Blakley Kinsler is the founder and past president of the Crochet Guild of America (CGOA). She has published articles on needlework and her own crochet design patterns. She is a Certified Craft Yarn Council of America Instructor and is committed to the importance of sharing her passion for crochet with anyone who is interested in learning, especially children. She coauthored *Crocheting—Kids Can Do It* (Kids Can Press, 2003).

Laurie Kimmelstiel is the coauthor of *Exquisite Little Knits* (Lark, 2004). Her work has been featured in *Handwoven* and *Ornament*. Laurie lives with her husband and three children in a home filled with yarn, looms, and pottery in White Plains, New York. She and her husband, a potter, exhibit their work through White Ridge Crafts www.whiteridgecrafts.com. You can reach Laurie at Kimmel.stiel@verizon.net

Katherine Lee is a Los Angeles-based designer. Her innovative designs have been published in many magazines and books, and purchased by thousands of crocheters and knitters through her website. She holds a degree in engineering and an MBA, but started www.SweaterBabe.com to combine her love of knitting and crochet into a full-time endeavor.

Ruthie Marks lives in Ojai, California. Her design work has been featured in many books and magazines including *Crocheted Scarves* (2003) in *Vogue Knitting's On the Go Series* and *Crochet Afghans* by Donna Kooler (Sterling, 2004).

Dot Matthews lives in Knightdale, North Carolina. She's retired with two grown sons and nine grandchildren. She enjoys crocheting items for charitable events: It gives her an outlet for her finished projects and a never-ending reason to crochet!

Donna May is a self-taught crochet veteran of over 40 years. For the past 20 years, she has been a hands-on healer and consulting astrologer as well. Though these disciplines may sound miles apart from crochet design, Donna will tell you they are more similar than different. She believes each is about patterns, cycles, creativity and harmony. Inspired by her grandchildren, Donna is currently developing a line of crochet patterns for infants and children.

Sue McCreary is from Erie, Pennsylvania. She's a CGOA member and her original designs have been featured in *Workbasket, Crochet Basket,* and other publications.

Marty Miller lives and teaches in Greensboro, North Carolina. She has been crocheting and creating her own patterns since she was a little girl. Her designs have appeared in magazines, books, and fashion shows, and in a major yarn company's pattern collections. She is a professional member and the Mentor Coordinator of the Crochet Guild of America (CGOA). When she is not crocheting or designing, Marty is a group exercise instructor and personal trainer at a local health club.

Nancy Minsky is a graduate of Parson's School of Design and the New School of Social Research. She's worked in the fashion industry for many years and has taught fashion design sketching at Parson's. She lives in Brussels with her conductor husband, Meir, and their family.

Lindsay Obermeyer lives in Chicago,Illinois. Her grandmother taught her to knit and crochet and she has used those lessons to create work that has been shown in Boston's Museum of Fine Arts and the Milwaukee Art Museum. Visit her website www.lbostudio.com

Barbara Zaretsky, a textile artist and graphic designer, has been creating wearable textile art for over 15 years. She specializes in surface design and needlework. Her designs have been featured in *Fiberarts* magazine and in boutiques, galleries, and craft shows. She's the cover director at Lark Books by day and crochets innovative hats in her spare time. The author of this book is wearing one on page 35.

Crochet Hook Sizes

Continental	U.S.
2.25 mm	B-1
2.75 mm	C-2
3.25 mm	D-3
3.5 mm	E-4
3.75 mm	F-5
4 mm	G-6
4.5 mm	7
5 mm	H-8
5.5 mm	I-9
6 mm	J-10
6.5 mm	K-10½
8 mm	L-11
9 mm	M/N-13
10 mm	N/P-15
15 mm	P/Q
16 mm	Q
19 mm	S

*Letter or number may vary by manufacturer. For accurate and consistent sizing, rely on the millimeter (mm) size.

Abbreviations

alt	alternate
Alt lp st	alternate loop stitch
approx	approximately
beg	begin, beginning
BL	back loop
BP	back post
Bbl st	Bobble stitch
ch	chain
ch-sp	chain space
cont	continue
dc	double crochet
dec	decrease(s/ing)
dtr	double treble crochet
ea	each
FL	front loop
FP	front post
hdc	half double crochet
hk	hook
inc	increase(s/ing)
lp(s)	loop(s)
Lp st	Loop stitch
oz	ounce(s)
prev	previous
rem	remaining
rep	repeat
reverse sc	reverse single crochet
RS	right side
rnd(s)	round(s)
sc	single crochet
sk	skip
sl st	slip stitch
sp	space(s)
st(s)	stitch(es)
tch	turning chain
tog	together
tr	treble crochet
Tss	Tunisian simple stitch
Tsl	Tunisian slip stitch
WS	wrong side
V-st	V- stitch
yo	yarn over

Index